Story of

WAR

Story of

WAR

by Robert Fox

BARNES
&NOBLE
BOOKS
NEW YORK

This edition published by Barnes & Noble, Inc. by arrangement with
Getty Images Publishing Projects,
Unique House, 21–31 Woodfield Road, London W9 2BA
email charles.merullo@gettyimages.com

For Getty Images:
Art director: Michael Rand
Design: Tea McAleer
Picture research: Slava Katamidze
Additional picture research: Ali Khoja
Editor: Sam Hudson
Proofreading and indexing: Liz Ihre
Special thanks: Elin Hagström, Mitch Blank, Valerie Zars and Francesca Kirby

Colour separation by @atColor Srl., Milan
Printed and bound by Nuovo Instituto Italiano D'Arti Grafiche, Bergamo, Italy

ISBN 0-7607-3567-0
M 10 9 8 7 6 5 4 3 2 1

frontispiece: American 3-inch anti-aircraft guns during
World War One.

CONTENT PAGE

WAR IN OUR TIME
the Changing Image

The 20th century was when global warfare came of age, mobilising and killing not just mass armies but civilians in their millions too, putting whole economies on a war footing, with fighting on land, on and under the sea and in the air. The scale and scope were beyond anything seen before, but the ways in which this warfare was reported and pictured, by war correspondents filing their stories by telegraph and using photography, had already become quite commonplace in the second half of the 19th century, starting with the Crimean War in 1854. William Howard Russell, one of the first modern war correspondents, who wrote for the London *Times* from the Crimea, described himself as, 'the miserable parent of a luckless tribe'. Kitchener called the reporters hanging round his head-quarters in Africa in the 1890s and 1900s 'drunken swabs'. Charles Page, one of the first American war correspondents, identified the root of their unpop-ularity. 'Correspondents', he wrote, 'will inevitably write things that offend somebody. Somebody will say harsh things of you, and set out to destroy you. Never mind. Such is part of the misery of correspondents.'

Writers and photographers did have an effect on political decision and public opinion from the beginning. Russell exposed the scandal of the condi-tions endured by the British soldiers in the Crimea, and this not only per-suaded Florence Nightingale to set up a nursing service and hospital at Scutari for them, but also did much to bring about the fall of the British gov-ernment. The newspapers on the Union side in the American Civil War are credited with persuading Lincoln and his staff to be niggardly with heavy artillery for the Union armies, keeping the best weaponry back for the defence of Washington DC itself, and only releasing it for the last campaign through the Wilderness, which was to bring the Confederate commander Robert E Lee's defeat and surrender in April 1865.

The photographs of Roger Fenton, who followed the British Army out to the Crimea in early 1855 were striking, and began to break down the accepted civilian image of war. Fenton could develop a plate in ten minutes in his horse-drawn darkroom. The team led by Matthew Brady in the American Civil War photographed the dead and the immediate aftermath of battles like Gettysburg, 1-3 July 1863, the bloodiest engagement of the war.

The age of the first war correspondents and photographers was also one of great technical innovation in the use of arms. Most significant was the advent of the rifled barrel for infantry firearms, and then of the all-in-one round, combining detonator, propulsive charge and pointed bullet. Artillery barrels were also rifled while breech-loading mechanisms for field guns and rifles gave greater rapidity of fire. The use of railways meant men and munitions could be delivered to the front in greater quantity and concentration. Technical innovation began to run ahead of the necessary modernisation in tactics, training, and even grand strategic thinking. The British and their allies developed the use of steamships and the telegraph in the Crimean War, but there was also almost breathtaking incompetence in logistical management and command. Nearly 50 years later the British Army came close to total defeat in South Africa at the hands of the Dutch farmers, the Boers, who, though inferior in numbers, showed greater skill in the use of terrain, manoeuvring in small commando groups, and in the use of modern rapid-fire rifles, which could operate at a range of 500 metres.

The problem posed by the new weaponry was described and depicted by professional reporters and photographers in the American Civil War. Russell was present at the pivotal battle of Königgrätz in 1866 when the Prussians defeated the Austrians thanks to their efficient mobilisation, and use of railways, and because they had the new breech-loading guns and all-in-one ammunition, giving them a much faster rate of fire than the Austrians. In the first three years of attrition on the Western Front in the First World War, modern rapid-fire weapons, artillery and rifles, later augmented by machine-guns, grenades and mortars, favoured well dug-in defence. From defence

trenches and well concealed artillery positions the defending army could control the 'killing zone' – the four to five hundred yards across which assaulting infantry would have to charge to seize a position. On the Western Front
this death zone was called No Man's Land. (In the American Civil War battle of Antietam, 17 September 1862 the killing zone was the Bloody Lane –
which the Confederates held until they inexplicably withdrew under Lee's
orders. Antietam was the single bloodiest day in the war.)

The lesson of defensive firepower was taught in the Boer War, the Russo-
Japanese War of 1904-1905 and in the two Balkan Wars of 1912-1913,
where huge armies, nearly a million strong on the Balkan League side, were
mobilised. The Russian Army, although defeated in 1905, did make some sur-

prising and lasting innovations, and was the first to use indirect artillery fire, ranged by observers well forward of the gun batteries themselves.

Despite the Germans' superiority at mobilisation, the war on the Western Front quickly became a murderous slogging match in 1914. Great poets such as Wilfred Owen, Siegfried Sassoon and Robert Graves have etched the terrible slaughter of the Somme battles and the Ypres Salient into modern memory. On the German side Erich Maria Remarque evoked the same experience in the classic novel *All Quiet on the Western Front*. Reporters' access to the front in the west was restricted by circumstances and censorship, though photographers and painters produced startling images – such as the photograph of blinded British gas victims at a dressing station, the inspiration of painter John Singer Sargent's masterpiece *Gas*. The huge casualties in Central and Eastern Europe, among the Russians and the Serbs, the Austrians and their allies, are not recorded so well as those on the

Western Front – though the attrition was relentless. It was enough to take Russia out of the war, and almost every army, except the British, mutinied.

Attrition was broken by the entry of novel weaponry and tactics, principally the tank and coordinated artillery fire plans, the 'creeping barrage' and observation of fire from aircraft. At Cambrai (Nov – Dec 1917) tanks of the new Royal Tank Corps were deployed *en masse* for the first time – and tore a ten-mile hole in the enemy lines. Equally significant for what was to come in the Second World War was the action on Messines Ridge in June 1917, where fire plans were coordinated for the first time on the Western Front so that the artillery fired on grid references and aircraft were used in combination with ground forces.

Aircraft and tanks opened the way for the fast-moving manoeuvre actions on almost all fronts in 1918. The British campaign of '100 days' through the summer brought success, largely due to superior staff work and preparation. The Australians, however, for all their courage and success, suffered greater casualties than in the previous years of attrition on the Western Front. In Palestine, combined air and ground attack effectively neutralised the retreating Turks.

The twenties and thirties were really a truce between the two world wars, but the bloodshed in Manchuria, China, Ethiopia and the Spanish Civil War shows they were far from peaceful. Hitler's generals were building the Panzer Divisions – manoeuvre units built round tanks. In 1937 at Guernica in the Spanish Civil War several waves of Heinkel 111 and Junkers 52 aircraft of the German Condor Legion bombed the town on market day, while Heinkel 51 fighters strafed fleeing refugees – a harbinger of what was to come in the German bombing and Blitzkrieg campaign in Western Europe. At the end of 1937 the Stuka dive-bomber first saw action with the Condor Legion. The 1930s saw developments in photography, too. Russians and Germans began using light, compact 35mm cameras, and movie cameras became more common on war fronts.

The Second World War was the first total war – with as many civilian casualties as among servicemen and women. In Russia more than 10 million civilians died, and the same number in China; Germany suffered 3.8 million civilian losses to 3.5 million military deaths. Industrial warfare reached its greatest volume, though even the German Wehrmacht relied on horsepower for its second-line logistics – and by 1943 there was a worldwide shortage of mules.

Operation Barbarossa, Hitler's invasion of Russia in June 1941, was the greatest single confrontation in the story of warfare. A total of 3 million Axis troops faced a Red Army of 4.5 million. Russia would eventually play the German Panzers at their own game. They had the best tank of the war in the T-34, which could manoeuvre quickly with its powerful engine and wide tracks, ideal for Russia's mud and snow, and be repaired and restored

Berlin, May 1945
A Russian 15-2 heavy tank, with the name 'Combat Girlfriend' written on it, in front of the Reichstag (parliament) building, from which the Red Flag flies.

to the battle line with astonishing efficiency and rapidity.

The war was fought by air and sea in a way which made it truly global – both the Pacific and the Atlantic were major theatres of action, with the great aircraft carrier battles in the Pacific in 1942, and the submarine campaign in the Atlantic, which nearly crippled Britain. From the air Britain and America initiated a strategic bombing campaign against German industry and communications, which meant huge civilian deaths, making it controversial to this day. The last big action of the war, the atomic bombing of Hiroshima and Nagasaki, marked the beginning of a new era. The concept of total destruction had been added to the concept of total war.

Savage Wars of Peace

Soon after peace came in 1945 Europe and the North Atlantic were locked in the long Cold War between the Soviet Union, founder and leader of the Warsaw Pact, and the United States and its allies in Nato. The alliances went beyond Europe and into the countries in Africa, the Middle East, South East Asia and Latin America looking for new, or renewed, nationhood and national liberation. The key feature of the Cold War was that the principals had nuclear weapons. The balance of peace was a balance of terror – the sure knowledge that one side could destroy the other, no matter who started it – a doctrine appropriately named MAD (Mutual Assured Destruction). Nuclear war between Russia and America only became a real possibility once – during the confrontation after America discovered Russia was building missile bases in Cuba in October 1962.

Apart from the Cold War, there were wars of decolonialisation and national liberation, insurrections and invasions, ideological and religious terror. Every year since 1945 a British service man or woman has died on operations.

In 1950 America and its allies confronted China's communist allies in North Korea, though the former fought under the banner of the United

Nations. Britain, France, the Netherlands and Portugal fought wars of decolonialisation, a political trauma which means they carry scars to this day. The British fought in places as diverse as Kenya, Aden, Borneo, Cyprus and Malaya. Its failure to curb the rise of the new socialist and nationalist hero of the Arab world, Gamal Abdul Nasser of Egypt, led to humiliation in the Suez crisis of 1956. Military honour, at least, was restored by victory over a failing Argentine military dictatorship in the Falklands-Malvinas conflict of 1982.

France was defeated in Vietnam when its military garrison was cut off and overwhelmed at Dien Bien Phu in 1954. After a bloody war of national liberation, in which up to a million people were killed and wounded, General de Gaulle pulled out of Algeria in 1962. The French Army was shaken by the mutiny of senior officers.

The American involvement in Vietnam, Cambodia and Laos, from 1961 to 1975, revealed warfare of a new order, involving huge physical and psychological loss. The Americans relied on combat power and technology, but many of the half million forces it sent to Asia over a decade were ill-prepared and reluctant conscripts. New weaponry, like helicopter gunships, were used for the first time. The Americans also waged war on the environment, defoliating jungles and forest to reveal the supply trails of the Vietcong and North Vietnamese Army. Huge damage was inflicted on the civilian population and its infrastructure, with 2 million Vietnamese killed, 3 million wounded. American losses were 55,000 dead and 150,000 wounded, proportionate to the numbers deployed, the worst casualties for US forces since the Civil War. The war became increasingly unpopular at home in the US, and led to huge demonstrations. Extensive coverage on television added to the mood of doubt – and the US generals and administration came to blame the hostile press for undermining support for the war.

Since 1945 warfare had become less formal and had taken a dramatic twist with a new breed of urban guerrilla and terrorist, autonomous even if sponsored by foreign powers. Britain faced urban terrorism in and from Northern

Ireland for 30 years; and Basque separatists from ETA have carried out an open-ended bombing and assassination campaign in Spanish cities.

The terrorist liberator became a subject for adulation among his people in popular comics, cartoons, and pulp journalism. Ernesto 'Che' Guevara, an Argentinian doctor, became a hero of the Communist revolution in Cuba, and tried to start a rising in Bolivia. After his death he became the radical icon of his age, though as a field commander he was a dismal failure. After the defeat of the Arab coalition by Israel in the Six-Day War, radical Palestinians joined guerrilla groups attached to the Palestinian Liberation Organisation and its affiliates. In

Suez, 1956
British troops on patrol in Port Said, Egypt.

1970 Palestinian guerrillas hijacked three airliners, and destroyed them at Dawson's Field, an empty airstrip in Jordan, after letting the passengers go free, which wouldn't happen too often in the future. This was the first of the 'spectacular' airline hijackings.

The Middle East Wars involving the state of Israel from its inception in 1948 had something of the old and something of the new. The Israelis used ground-air tactics – rapid armoured advance combined with air strikes – in its sweeping victories in the Six-Day War of 1967 and again in 1973. But in their cities and settlements they faced attacks by car bombs, first used by insurgents in Algeria, sniping, assassination and the suicide bomber.

The Cold War in Europe ended with a whimper, not a bang. The Berlin Wall fell in November 1989, and Communism in eastern Europe was over. The surprise was that for all their military might, the Soviet forces withdrew from their advance positions in Germany and its neighbours peacefully and in good order.

New World Disorder 1989 – 2001

The Cold War gave way to a hot peace. The Nato and Warsaw Pact powers had expected a respite, a reduction of their forces, and 'a peace dividend'. But within a year of the fall of the Berlin Wall they found themselves lining up against a common foe in a conventional form of war – though with a very unconventional overtone, following Iraq's seizure of Kuwait in August 1990. Operation Desert Storm proved a rerun of the conventional air-land battle. The allies had more than 400,000 troops in the Eastern Desert, which drove the Iraqi forces out of Kuwait in 100 hours. It was perhaps the last conventional armoured battle involving massed tanks, however one-sided, even though it involved less than one seventh of the armoured and air forces taking part in Hitler's Invasion of Russia in June 1941.

In 1991 war came to Europe in the series of conflicts arising from the disintegration of the old Communist Yugoslav Federation. Again conventional weapons were used to cause terror in an unconventional way, civilian populations were moved, made prisoner and even massacred. The old slogans of racial purification lived once more in the campaigns of murder justified by

the term 'ethnic cleansing'.

Africa was to see dreadful wars of ethnic cleansing. In Rwanda, hundreds of thousands of the Tutsi minority were butchered after a coup in 1994 – and more misery, killings and expulsions were to follow.

The World and War after September 11

On 7 August 1998 bombs exploded at the American Embassies in Nairobi and Dar-es Salaam, killing 257, most of them Africans. The outrage focussed attention on the al Qaeda organisation of the Saudi dissident Osama bin Laden. America launched cruise missiles at a factory in Sudan and training camps in Afghanistan, where bin Laden had been guest of the repressive Taliban regime. Little was known about al Qaeda, and so America and the world were little prepared for the events of 11 September 2001.

The attacks on the Pentagon and the World Trade Center marked a new phase in terrorist warfare, as a few men intent on martyrdom turned four aircraft into flying bombs and struck the symbolic centres of American finance and defence. It was an act of asymmetric warfare: a weak and unknown adversary strikes an opponent at its most vulnerable point – David against Goliath. The aims of bin Laden are shadowy and obscure – and seem as much in the mind as having anything to do with the politics of this world. Yet his stance has a powerful appeal to the disinherited poor of the burgeoning Islamic world.

The rules of warfare are being rewritten. Clausewitz's recipe of wars made by peoples, governments and armies has been turned on its head. War is now made among the people and by men neither elected nor sanctioned by law. Wars are no longer governed by time, and limitation of arms and material. Conflict is open-ended and unpredictable. The media, which set out to report events and actions to a civilised audience, are now seen as instruments and weapons in the new conflict. Some see this post-modern conflict as the Third World War.

The Crimean War

The image of war changed utterly in the mid-19th century with the War in the Crimea (1853-1856) and the American Civil War (1861-1865), as they began to be reported by professional correspondents, war artists and photographers. The realities of violent death were brought home to ordinary people for the first time by photographs of corpses strewn on Civil War battlefields.

Britain and France sent expeditions to preserve their ally, the Turkish empire, by attacking the Russian fortifications on the Crimean Peninsula in the Black Sea – the key being the heavily fortified port of Sebastopol. Though there were some steamships, logistics and supply were a shambles. Infamously one ship arrived with a consignment of left boots only. More British soldiers died of disease than were killed by the enemy.

The most celebrated incident of the war, perhaps, was the suicidal charge of Lord Cardigan's Light Brigade at the Battle of Balaclava. William Howard Russell of *The Times* recorded the loss of 247 men out of 670 in 20 minutes: 'their desperate valour knew no bounds, and far indeed was it removed from its so-called better part – discretion.'

The newsman's despatch could now be relayed by telegraph and appear in newspapers in days rather than weeks or months. Roger Fenton with his mobile darkroom could develop his pictures in 10 minutes, like that of the French General Bosquet and his staff (right). It was Bosquet who made the famous remark about the Charge of the Light Brigade, that it was magnificent but not proper war.

The epic siege of Sebastopol, the centrepiece of the war, lasted a year, to September 1855. On the ramparts was a young Russian officer, Leo Tolstoy, and his experiences became ingredients of the battle scenes in his masterpiece *War and Peace*.

Balaclava Harbour
The sheltered inlet with
the ruins of an old castle
built by the Genoese in
the background. All the
supplies for the armies
besieging Sebastopol had
to be landed here. The
flow of food, clothing,
ammunition, etc. often
broke down and news of
this became a national
scandal at home in
Britain. Later in the
war a railway was built
to take them to the
troops above.

At the siege of Sebastopol

Colonel Shadforth parades the 57th Regiment, Crimea
War, 1855 (above). The interior of the Redan Fort after
the fall of Sebastopol in September 1855 (right). It was
one of the strong points of the Russian defences, and
defeated two British assaults on it. In the two attacks,
the British lost more than 4,000 dead. It was eventually
overwhelmed by French troops.

Images of War

The photographer Roger Fenton in the uniform of a French Zouave soldier (above) and his mobile darkroom (below) used in the Crimean War. The encampment of the 97th Light Infantry (right) before the last attacks on Sebastopol in September 1855.

Off duty

A French vivandière, who sold food and drink to the
men (above). Officers of 42nd Highlanders, now the
Black Watch (below). The 4th Dragoons pour a drink
for a visiting French soldier (right).

The American Civil War

The American Civil War (1861-1865) was to prove the bloodiest and most innovative war of its century. Steamships, telegraphs, spotter balloons, railways, and massed artillery were deployed. Guns like the siege mortar 'Dictator' of the Union Army, seen at Petersburg, Virginia in 1864 (right), were vital. Ostensibly, about slavery, it was the clash of the more languid land-based south against the burgeoning industrial economy of the north. More Americans died on the battlefields of the Civil War than the total killed in all subsequent wars, until Vietnam. Nearly every family would be affected by the slaughter, in which more than 600,000 soldiers on both sides died.

Military advantage at first was with the 11 states of the southern Confederacy which had fewer men, about 110,000 to the North's 150,000 initially, but better generals – in particular Robert E Lee, 'Stonewall' Jackson, and James Longstreet. However, the South was at a severe disadvantage over manpower and resources, with a population of 9 million to the 25 million of the North. The decisive battle was Gettysburg in 1863, where General Robert E Lee made the error of ordering troops to charge across open ground on Cemetery Ridge on the last day. They were sliced to ribbons in a matter of minutes, a clear demonstration of concentrated firepower from modern weaponry. Union forces had suffered in the same way on the Bloody Lane at Antietam in 1862.

Both Lee and his opposing commander in chief, Ulysses S Grant, learnt from these incidents the arts of manoeuvre warfare, bypassing and outflanking obstacles to reach the final objective. These lessons would be forgotten by the time the First World War broke out.

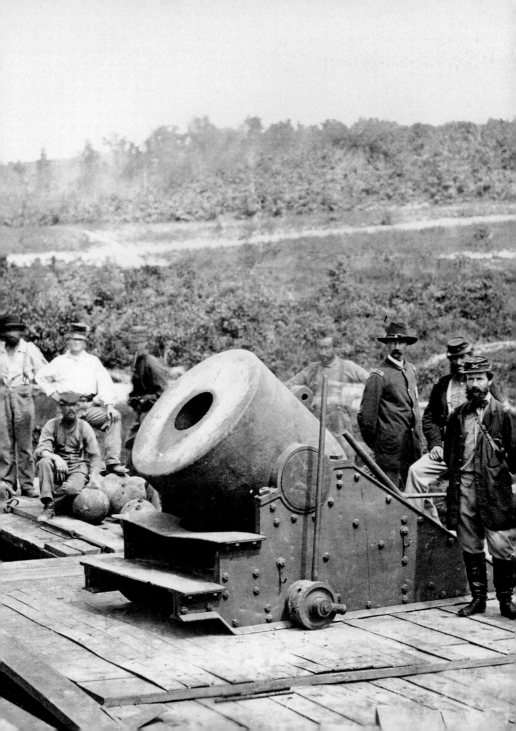

Count Zeppelin

The Count (above, second right), from Germany, on a battlefield tour in 1863 with officers of the Union Army. Many gentleman observers and correspondents visited the war, among them William Russell of *The Times*.

On parade

The 96th Pennsylvania Regiment drilling at Camp Northumberland outside Washington DC in 1861, the opening year of the war (left). Most Union troops were untried, though supplies of recruits were unlimited compared with the South.

Matthew Brady, War Photographer

The 'Whatsit Waggon', the mobile darkroom (above) of
one of Matthew Brady's team of photographers.
Matthew Brady (1823-1896) (below). The Union Army
of the Potomac artillery park at Yorktown, Virginia
(right), a Brady photograph from 1862.

Men at arms

General William Tecumseh Sherman (1820-1891), one
of the most successful of the North's commanders.
However, his march through Georgia to Savannah in
1864, which he started with the razing of Atlanta before
laying waste to all in his path, was to cause resentment
for generations to come. A Powder Monkey, on the
Union warship *New Hampshire* off the coast of South
Carolina (right). These boys kept the guns supplied with
powder charges. Both sides experimented with ironclad
warships – the *Merrimack* and the *Monitor* – and primitive submarines.

The dead
Confederate soldier in
the trench lines at
Fredricksburg, Virginia
towards the end of hos-
tilities (left), taken by
Thomas C Roche, one
of Brady's photogra-
phers who often
improved their shots by
arranging or adding
weaponry, as here.

Blood and Iron: Germany Unites

General Helmuth von Moltke, Chief of the German General Staff, and his armies were to influence war and strategy more than any others in the 19th century. In a series of short wars, against Denmark, Austria and finally France, Germany was united under the Iron Chancellor, Bismarck, and became a new European empire. Prussians can be seen after taking the Danish fortress of Duppel in 1864 (right).

Austria then unwisely picked a fight, leading to the Seven Weeks' War of 1866. Von Moltke manoeuvred three armies across an arc of 270 miles from Saxony to Silesia. The decisive battle was at Königgrätz outside Sadowa on the Elbe. The use of railways and the superior breech-loading 'needle guns' helped the Prussians carry the day. But the Austrians under Count Benedek, though losing 40,000 as casualties and prisoners, fought a gallant retreat, aided by superior artillery.

Von Moltke remedied weaknesses in logistics and artillery, with the assistance of Herr Krupp's breech-loading guns, by the Franco-Prussian War of 1870-1871 – when France tried to arrest Prussia's growing power. In 18 days the Germans delivered 380,000 men to the front. At the beginning of September 1870, after the decisive battle of Sedan, Napoleon III surrendered with 85,000 troops, and in October an even larger French army surrendered in Metz. Paris came under siege which lasted until 28 January 1871, despite the attempts of Léon Gambetta to rally France after escaping the capital by balloon.

Radical Paris then decided to declare itself an autonomous Commune, inviting other cities to follow. In late May 1871 the French army took on the 'Fédérés' militia and the Commune was defeated in the 'bloody week', *la semaine sanglante*, in which 20,000 communards died.

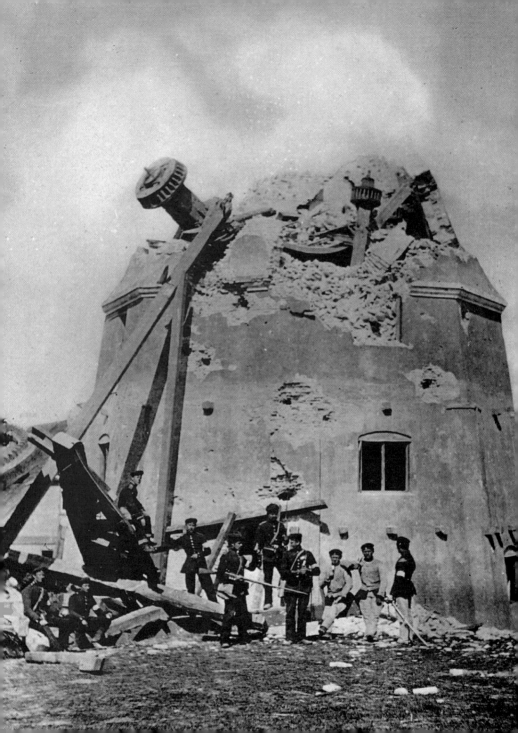

War in Denmark
Prussian and Austrian forces set up camp in the ruins of the Danish fort at Duppel after it had been overrun, summer 1864. Germany began the process of unification with this rather obscure war under Prussian command. However, the Prussian army nearly lost it in the opening stages, and victories like this were only achieved after an unusual and daring amphibious attack.

The Battle of Sedan

The Prussian advance in the early stages of the battle of
Sedan, September 1870. One of the first photographs
showing a battle in progress. The Prussians won the battle through their well-directed artillery, a lesson their
commander, von Moltke, had learnt in the war of 1866
against Austria.

Escape by balloon

A balloon being inflated at Place St Pierre Montmartre for a reconnaissance mission – just as the siege of Paris is beginning, 23 September 1870. Léon Gambetta was to escape the siege in a similar balloon to rally resistance in the rest of France. The photographer Nadar, a pioneer of ballooning in the Paris siege, poses (above) in a balloon gondola rigged in his studio,1875.

Paris, March 1871
Prussian infantry and
horse artillery, part of a
victory parade in the
French capital after the
end of the Franco-
Prussian War.

The Paris Commune
Aux Armes
Communards! A barricade at Porte Maillot,
the Arc de Triomphe in
the distance, taken during the 'bloody week' of
the Commune,
May 1871.

The Balkans

A series of rebellions and wars ended Ottoman Turk rule in all but a slice of Europe: Greece won independence in 1832 and, following the Russo-Turkish War of 1877-8, Serbia, Montenegro and Romania won theirs at the Congress of Berlin. One of the most remarkable states to emerge was tiny Montenegro, which had previously enjoyed extensive freedom under its prince-bishops of the Petrovic-Njegos family.

The Berlin Congress brought peace to the Balkans for a generation – though Serbia was racked by bloody palace revolution. In 1908 Austria annexed Bosnia-Hercegovina, a lasting grudge for Serbian nationalists, since many of the inhabitants were Serb. In 1912 Serbia with its allies in the Balkan League, Bulgaria, Greece and Montenegro, fought Turkey for the liberation of Macedonia and Thrace. Huge armies were involved – the League called just under a million to arms, and put armies of 700,000 in the field. Perhaps among them was Katrina Asariantova, a 'famous partisan', probably Serbian, photographed in 1906 (right). The Bulgarians advanced on Istanbul, and Greece attacked the Turks in Macedonia. Istanbul held, but Adrianople fell. No sooner was peace made in May 1913 than the allies rounded on Bulgaria over Macedonia. Bulgaria attempted a pre-emptive strike against the Greeks and Serbs, but failed. Turkey retook Adrianople, and on 29 July 1913 Bulgaria sued for peace.

The wars in the Balkans foreshadowed what was soon to come in the Great War of 1914-18. Both sides used 1,000 machineguns between them, relied on entrenchments, and prepared for aerial attack. On 28 June 1914, a Serb nationalist murdered the Austrian heir Franz Ferdinand in Sarajevo, the Bosnian capital. The machinery of mass mobilisation pioneered by von Moltke's staff officers and their peers across Europe was set into motion and no one seemed to know how to apply the brake.

News from the front

Serbian soldiers read of the Turkish counter-offensive
under Mustapha Pasha, 1913. The Balkan wars were
extensively photographed and heavily reported by professional correspondents, including Leon Trotsky.

Royal embrace

King Nicholas of Montenegro is greeted by one of his
soldiers, 8 October 1912, in the First Balkan War. The
historic capital, Cetinje, is still intact, a model of its
kind, with wonderful embassies built at the time this
photograph was taken.

Balkan weaponry

A field gun of the Bulgarian army before Adrianople in
the aftermath of the Second Balkan War, August 1913.
Adrianople had been taken in the First Balkan War by
the Bulgarians, only to be lost to the Turks in the second. An officer uses an upturned limber as a stand from
which to 'spot' for his battery of Krupp guns.

Posed shots

Balkan soldiers in 1906 – quite clearly staged as their
clothes are astonishingly clean. They are probably from
the Serbian army, from the crest in their caps, and they
have modern bolt action rifles with magazines.

India and China

Russian and British armies never confronted each other as they expanded into Asia, but Britain was to fight three wars in Afghanistan, a buffer state which could easily fall to the Russians. The first war of 1838-42 saw the infamous 'Retreat from Kabul' in which the British garrison was massacred by Pathan tribesmen, like these (right). In the Second Afghan War (1878-1880) General 'Bobs' Roberts had to mount a daring expedition to Kandahar to restore British influence, then Britain had to organise an evacuation of its nationals by air following a Third Afghan War in 1919.

In 1857 native Indian troops, sepoys, of the Bengal Army revolted, and British officers and civilians in garrisons across India came under attack. It was a revolt with many causes, the chief being British over-confidence which led to them giving too much offence to too many influential elements in Indian society. Retribution was brutal: a favourite punishment, learnt from the Moghul rulers who preceded the British, was to strap mutineers to cannon mouths and blow them apart.

Equally tough measures were taken by the British to maintain their commercial interests in South East Asia and China. In 1900 anti-western nationalists known as 'Boxers' rebelled in China, with the connivance of the Chinese dowager Empress, and were defeated eventually by a grand alliance of powers. In August 1900 western troops entered the Forbidden City in Beijing. The crushing of the revolt led to the end of the Manchu dynasty in 1911. At the same time as the Boxer Rebellion, Britain was at war in South Africa against the Boers.

The Mutiny
An Akali Sikh who fought in the Indian Mutiny, 1858 (left). One of the numerous mosques within the walls of Delhi (above), the old capital of Moghul India and centre of resistance to the British during the Mutiny, until it fell in September 1857. Artillerymen pose in front of the city wall with their gun, which probably helped to batter it. Pictures by Felice Beato, a pioneer photographer.

The Mutiny: Lucknow

The Chutter Munzil Palace (above), one of several in
Lucknow destroyed when the city was finally stormed
by troops under Sir Colin Campbell in March 1858.
Native officers of Hodson's Horse (right), an irregular
unit raised by Captain William Hodson to fight in the
Mutiny for the British. Hodson shot two sons of the
King of Delhi out of hand at the end of the siege there
and was himself killed in the final assault on Lucknow.

Second Afghan War
Troops under General
Sir Frederick 'Bobs'
Roberts man the
defences at Kabul. The
British advanced twice
on Kabul during the war
and, in the process, gave
Roberts, who had won
the Victoria Cross dur-
ing the Indian Mutiny,
the status of public hero.

Spoils of war

General Sir Frederick 'Bobs' Roberts (centre, astride
white horse) inspects captured enemy artillery at
Kandahar, 1880. His dramatic 300-mile march from
Kabul to Kandahar brought an end to the war.

Defeat of the Boxers: China 1900

Victorious allies: representatives of the German, British, French, Italian, American and Russian forces in Beijing after the defeat of the Boxer Rebellion 1900 (above). US cavalrymen (right) at the Great Wall of China during the Boxer Rebellion, and German cavalry arriving at the walls of Beijing after the rebels have been crushed (left).

Scramble for Africa

From the 1870s there developed something of a race between European powers to colonise Africa. Warfare between them was avoided, but there was plenty of fighting with the indigenous peoples. Britain assumed responsibility for Egypt and Sudan, heavily indebted to French and British banks. In 1881 there was a serious rebellion under Arabi Pasha, a former Army officer. The British fleet bombarded Alexandria after about 50 Europeans were killed in riots there in 1882 and then Sir Garnet Wolseley's expeditionary force defeated the rebels at Tel-el-Kebir. Scottish soldiers from it pose in front of the Sphinx after the victory (right).

Wolseley was immortalised as 'the very model of a modern major-general' by Gilbert and Sullivan. However, the column he ordered to Khartoum during a rebellion of Sudanese 'dervishes' – fanatical Islamic followers of one of many self-proclaimed Mahdis (saviours) – did not get there in time and his friend General Gordon was murdered in his headquarters. The rebellion in Sudan was finally brought to an end by an expeditionary force under Herbert Horatio Kitchener at the Battle of Omdurman in 1898 when the 21st Lancers, including the young Winston Churchill, carried out one of the last serious charges by British cavalry. The British Maxim guns (machineguns) made victory desperately one-sided – the British suffered 43 dead and 428 wounded, to at least 9,700 Sudanese dead and 16,000 wounded.

In the earlier Zulu War, a Zulu Impi overran an expeditionary force, commanded by Lord Chelmsford at Isandhlwana on the night of 22 January 1879, killing 1,329 British and native forces. On the same night another Zulu force attacked the tiny British garrison at Rorke's Drift. They held out till dawn, suffering only 15 killed to more than 500 Zulu dead. Eleven of the group won the highest gallantry decoration, the Victoria Cross – the most for any single battle.

Alexandria 1882

The campaign against Arabi Pasha opened with the bombardment of Alexandria – to maintain Britain's grip on Egypt and the vital link through the Suez Canal to India. British sailors pose on the ramparts with antiquated Egyptian artillery (left), and with the British fleet in the harbour. Destruction from the brief bombardment of Alexandria by the British fleet (above).

War in the Sudan

War to secure Sudan
went on until 1900.
Here Australian officers
rest their forces during
the 1899 campaign at
Hadoub. The figure in
the right foreground has
a heliograph, a signalling
device consisting of a
pivoting mirror which
reflects the sun's rays so
as to transmit messages
in Morse code.

Zulu war

Soldiers of the Natal Native Contingent (left) raised to fight for the British. Some 500 were killed at Isandhlwana. Men of 'B' Company 2/24th South Wales Borderers (above) after the defence of Rorke's Drift on the night of 22/23 January 1879. A total of 140 men held out against 4,000 Zulus.

The Spanish-American War

The United States, like the European powers, suffered from imperial urges and, in what was described as 'a splendid little war', in 1898 went on the offensive and acquired a clutch of 'dependencies' in the Pacific and control over Cuba and Puerto Rico in the Caribbean.

Insurgents had been fighting the Spanish imperial authorities in Cuba and the Philippines for some years, when President McKinley decided to offer them Washington's overt support in 1898, pushed into action by a jingoistic press campaign. Washington was also concerned at the rounding up of some 100,000 Cubans into 'concentration camps' (the first use of the term). On 15 February 1898 the US battlecruiser *Maine* blew up in Havana harbour, and war was declared, without waiting to find out the reason for the explosion.

In the Philippines Commodore Dewey destroyed a Spanish squadron without any loss of American lives on May 1, though there were fatalities ashore later, as testified to by this picture of three dead American soldiers on the side of a Philippine road (right). The Spanish in the Caribbean and Pacific could not match the new American battle fleets – and also had difficulty in getting supplies of fuel coal. An expeditionary force from Tampa, Florida landed in Cuba in the summer and by August Spanish resistance was all but crushed. By the Treaty of Paris, the USA was allowed to annex Guam, Puerto Rico and the Philippines – and given widespread rights of oversight of the new nationalist government in Cuba, as well as a naval base at Guantanamo Bay there. The hero of the war was Theodore Roosevelt, the future president, who led his 'Rough Riders' in battles at Santiago and at Kettle's Hill in Cuba. The Americans lost 385 dead in the war, and 2,061 from disease.

Volunteers and rebels

The press had whipped up powerful backing for the war. Volunteers cheer as they leave San Francisco aboard the transport *Rio de Janeiro* to join US forces in Manila (left). Cuban rebels cook a pig in their jungle hideout (above). The rebels won independence, up to a point, since Cuba was to remain under the thumb of the US until 1959.

Washington volunteers
Looking like the shootout in some Western movie, this is in fact American soldiers firing as they advance in Cuba (above).

Execution in Cuba
The Spanish were accused of widespread atrocities, including the use of concentration camps to hold suspected rebel sympathisers. Here six prisoners are lined up for the firing squad (left).

The Boer War

This was the biggest challenge to British forces since the Indian Mutiny, bringing them to the brink of defeat. In October 1899, the Dutch farmers ('Boers') of the Transvaal and the Orange Free State, fearing their states were about to be swallowed by Britain, sent forces into Natal, besieging the frontier towns of Ladysmith, Mafeking and Kimberley on the way. The Boers had the edge from the beginning. They were excellent shots, well equipped with small arms, and superb in field craft and intelligence out on the veldt, the open grasslands. Age was no barrier to serving, as this picture, including a 15- and a 65-year-old, testifies (right). Their biggest weakness was in artillery.

In December in 'Black Week', the Boers inflicted three stunning defeats on the British forces commanded by Sir Redvers Buller, at Magersfontein, Stormberg and Colenso. In January Buller was again defeated at Spion Kop, where British Imperial troops fought valiantly for a rocky feature, which the Boers successfully counterattacked.

The Boer armies soon ran out of steam, lacking resupplies and manpower. The British Army and tactics were reformed under Lord Roberts and his chief of staff, General Kitchener, to meet the skilful hit-and-run raids. After the relief of Ladysmith, Kimberley and Mafeking, Roberts won a significant victory at Diamond Hill in June 1900, and the war appeared almost over. But for 15 months the Boers mounted a series of brilliant guerrilla and sabotage campaigns.

Kitchener built thousands of blockhouses and burnt the farms of Boers away fighting. More than 100,000 women and children were rounded up in concentration camps – built on the model of those in the recent war in Cuba. Conditions were appalling and tens of thousands died from disease. By 1902 the Boers were exhausted and were granted generous surrender terms in the Treaty of Vereeniging.

Defence and attack

Boer soldiers man forward trenches in the siege of
Mafeking, 1900 (above), armed with German Mauser
rifles, They could shoot accurately at ranges over 500
yards, and were more than a match for the British Lee
Enfields. Canadian soldiers climb a *kopje* (right), in the
battle for Sunnyside Farm, 1900.

Casualty treatment

An Indian auxiliary undergoing surgery at the open-air field hospital run by Major Ford at Paordelerg. In the course of the war, 8,000 British were killed in action. But another 13,000 Britons and 15,000 non-whites, died from disease or malnutrition.

Wounded Boers
Prisoners of war at Wijnberg Hospital, Pretoria. 4,000
Boers were killed in action and another 30,000 died of
disease or malnutrition.

Bombing the Boers
A British 4.7 inch naval gun, nicknamed 'Joe Chamberlain' after the Colonial Secretary who took the country into the Boer War. It is firing at Boer positions in Magersfontein in 1900.

Parley

A blindfolded German intermediary is escorted through British lines to negotiate a surrender at Modder River Camp, 17 March 1900. It was at this stage that the Boers were switching from manoeuvring armies in the field to a guerrilla campaign. The Germans were very pro-Boer and the Kaiser would have intervened, had he possessed the necessary naval strength to confront the Royal Navy.

Dry and out

Canadian, Australian and New Zealand infantry on the
march after the occupation of Brandfort where Roberts'
armies rounded up 4,000 Boer prisoners in the summer
of 1900 (left). Boer artillery being moved up for the
siege of Ladysmith, 1899 (above). Ladysmith was
relieved on 28 February 1900. The Boer bombardment
there had been largely ineffective because it always
happned at the same time of day, so the besieged could
take cover in advance.

Armoured Rehearsal

At the beginning of the 20th century, there was a surprising contest between Japan and Russia, over interests in Manchuria, Korea and the newly acquired Russian Pacific base of Port Arthur. Both sides fought to a standstill on land, the Russians under such commanders as General Linerich, seen in Manchuria (right). Then the Russians decided to send ships from the Baltic to reinforce their Pacific Squadron. The force entered the Straits of Tsushima between Korea and Japan on 27 May 1905 when the Japanese fleet destroyed all eight battleships of the Baltic Squadron and the armoured cruisers, and won the war. In defeat Russia agreed to give up Port Arthur, and Korea passed into the Japanese sphere of influence. In the ground war the Russians had used artillery in an indirect fire mode for the first time – and barbed wire and entrenchments were also used extensively, heralding the tactics of the First World War.

When Italy and Turkey fought over Libya between 1911 and 1912 aircraft were also used for reconnaissance and bombing Turkish lines – an innovation adopted by Bulgaria during the Balkan Wars of 1912-13. Turkey gave up its Libyan provinces in 1912.

At the same time the future Marshal Lyautey was establishing the French protectorate in Morocco. In 1925 this was to be severely challenged by Abd el-Krim, encouraged to invade by his victory in Spanish Morocco at Amial in the Riff in 1921.

In North America two legendary figures became embroiled in the most curious neo-colonial war of the time. Pancho Villa, the peasants' leader who led the overthrow in 1911 of President Diaz of Mexico, ending his 45-year rule, became involved in a guerrilla raid on Columbus in New Mexico. US General John J Pershing led a punitive expedition and destroyed the rebel camp, using aircraft to track down the rebels.

War in Manchuria

Japanese troops in battle order. The uniforms are still
highly ceremonial, reflecting the idea of warrior caste,
the Samurai, though interestingly the officer's sword is
of European pattern.

Taking post
Russian troops manning earthworks and revetments after the alarm has been sounded by the drummers on the left. This kind of fortification was a forerunner of the trench systems of the First World War.

Defeat

Russian prisoners of war after the Japanese victory at
Talien in Manchuria (above). The Japanese treated their
prisoners in an exemplary way in this war, in contrast to
their behaviour in later ones. A stockpile of 11-inch
high-explosive shells (right) for Japanese siege artillery
used against Russian ships and forts.

Taking refuge

The Russian battleship *Tzarevitch* in the German treaty
port of Kiaochau in China (above). Damage to the fun-
nel can be seen clearly. Eight other Russian battleships
were sunk in the battle of Tsushima on 27-28 May,
1905. The port of Yokohama (right) decked out to cele-
brate Admiral Togo's victory at Tsushima.

France and Spain in Morocco

A French observation balloon being taken to the front, in Morocco (left). Moorish gunners about to attack the Spanish colonial army in Spanish Morocco, 1923 (above).

War in North Africa
General Saro advancing
through the hills of
Malmusi to take
Axdis, 1925.

On the march
Italian troops advance against Turkish forces in Libya, c. 1911. They do not look dressed for the heat of North Africa.

Turkey versus Italy

A contingent of the Turkish army marches through
Constantinople before embarking for Libya. They are
led by a mounted band complete with kettle drums,
instruments which western armies adopted from the
Turks some centuries before.

Running repairs

A member of the Italian Bersaglieri having a hand injury
dressed on the way to Libya, 1911. The troops, including the doctor, are mounted on modern bicycles, however quaint their cocks' feather plumes, and they have
goggles against the dust.

Mexican revolution

Casualties in the Grand Plaza, Mexico City, 1913
(above). In 1911 Pancho Villa and Emiliano Zapata
overthrew President Porfirio Diaz, who had ruled for 45
years. A series of revolutions took place in 1911, 1913,
and 1915, when Villa and Zapata were defeated.
Guadalupe Candeleria (right), the 15-year-old hero of
the 1913 revolution who recovered the injured and
dying from the thick of the fighting in Mexico City.

The American-Mexican War 1916
General John Pershing leading the punitive expedition
against Pancho Villa after he had mounted a raid on
Columbus, New Mexico.

Pancho Villa

Villa in characteristic pose. He overthrew President
Diaz but was then defeated by his successor, President
Carranza. Villa raided the USA as punishment for
helping Carranza.

FIRST WORLD WAR

Stalemate

The Great War opened on a tide of patriotic enthusiasm and most thought it would be brief. Units marched off behind bands, with something of the swagger displayed by the *pickelhaube*-helmeted goose-stepping German soldier (right).

The Germans aimed at a swift thrust in the west to neutralise France before tackling the huge enemy in the east, Russia, which mobilised more than 12 million men. The strike into France was halted east of Paris by French and British forces on the Marne in early September 1914. Soon the war had settled to a long slogging match, as the use of trenches and barbed wire and the domination of artillery, mortars and machineguns across the killing zone of no-man's land led to stalemate for three and a half years. In the east Russia, having first driven back the German and Austrian armies, suffered heavy defeat.

The arithmetic of the killing still makes chilling reading – the British lost just under 20,000 killed and 40,000 injured and missing on 1 July 1916, the first day of the Somme offensive. That year there were 750,000 French and German casualties at Verdun. The following year half the French army refused orders to attack after the botched offensive of the Chemin des Dames in Champagne, which forced the British to try another push at Passchendaele.

New weapons like mines and poison gas were used by both sides to break the deadlock. But this would only happen when artillery could be fully coordinated with infantry attacks. The tank and aircraft brought new mobility to the battlefield, and the United States entered the war in 1917, compensating for the collapse of the Russians into revolution. Some of the American 'doughboys' met a swift end, like the one on the wire (previous page).

Trench warfare

French troops recovering bodies from a communication trench on the Western Front, 1915 (left). Canadian machinegunners at Passchendaele, November 1917 (above). The battle opened in July, but torrential rain in August and the destruction of the field drains by the artillery barrage meant that soldiers, horses and mules drowned in mud.

The Eastern Front

Russian guns on the Eastern Front, 1914. They are firing in direct line of sight, the fall of shot observed by the man with binoculars. The aircraft at this early stage of the war would not have been in communication with the ground.

**Guns on the Somme
1916**
Heavy artillery of the
British 39th Siege
Battery firing in the
Fricourt-Mametz sector
in the battle of the
Somme, August 1916.
The battle was now a
long slog and would run
into November 1916.
The man with out-
stretched arm has just
pulled the lanyard
attached to the firing
mechanism. Each gun
has a small crane by it to
hoist up the heavy shells.

Poilus

A French soldier, a 'poilu', throws what looks like a
land mine from the top of his trench redoubt during the
Somme offensive in 1916.

The Austrian Army

Machinegunners in action in the Carso – the rocky area in which they fought the Italians, now in Slovenia, 1917. Soon they would go on the offensive, routing the Italians at Caporetto between 24 October and 7 November 1917.

Gas, the Western Front

The Germans and the British used several varieties of
gas, which they released from cylinders as well as shells.
Much depended on the direction of the wind – which
could make attackers vulnerable if it changed. A
German officer (above) leads his men through a cloud
of phosphene gas, released to cover their attack on
British trenches, the Somme 1916. Gas victims,
Béthune, France 1 April 1918 (right). These British soldiers have been blinded by mustard gas: one of the most
famous images of the war, and the inspiration for John
Singer Sargent's painting *Gas*.

Movement

The British used the first tanks a on the Somme in September, 1916, then at Cambrai in November 1917 where 378 broke a wide hole to a depth of 5 miles. The attack was not followed up, however. British Tommies hitch a lift (right).

In March 1918 the Germans used new tactics: forward units of 'storm troopers' equipped with machine guns and flame-throwers to bypass and envelop enemy strong points. The attack outran its supply lines and was checked by the Allies, now under the coordinated command of Marshal Foch. Using tanks and aircraft as bombers, he struck back at the Second Battle of the Marne and at Amiens. Ludendorff called 8 August the 'black day' for the German army. An armistice was signed on 11 November.

The war at sea was a global affair. The German Pacific Squadron was all but wiped out off the Falklands in December 1914. In 1915 the British cruiser squadron under Beatty engaged a German cruiser group and the battle cruiser *Blücher* sunk on the Dogger Bank. The biggest engagement was at Jutland in 1916. The British sustained heavier losses, but forced the German fleet to port for the rest of the war. In 1917 Germany stepped up the offensive by submarines – declaring merchant ships would be sunk without warning. This brought America into the war in April 1917, a month in which German submarines sank 820,000 tons of British shipping.

Aircraft were used for bombing from the beginning of the war. But they only fought each other from 1916 onwards, and then at the Somme were used for coordinating artillery fire, communicating with the ground by radio. In 1917 the first German Gotha bombers hit London. Aircraft combined with armoured cars and mounted infantry, under the command of General Allenby, to defeat the Turks in the Levant.

German break-through

German 'storm troop-ers', part of Luden-dorff's offensive Michael in March 1918, attack the French near Villers-Bretonneux. It had great success but stalled for lack of supplies.

Air war

A French pilot makes a precarious take-off from a
ploughed field during training (above). A dead British
pilot next to his downed aircraft, under German gaze,
1915 (right).

Observation and aerial photography

Aerial reconnaissance on the Western Front was carried out by balloons at first. Here the French prepare to launch one in 1915 (left). More and more use was made of aerial photography as the war went on, like this shot of a devastated French or Belgian town (above).

Air weapons
A bomb released from a German biplane (right). The
bombs would be dropped by hand by the co-pilot. Using
guns effectively on aircraft was difficult at first because
they were fitted to single swivel mountings. The
German air gunner here has his gun on a swivel
anchored to a rotating ring – giving a much broader
field of fire (above).

Gallipoli.
Allied troops landing at
ANZAC Cove, Gallipoli
Peninsula. The amphibi-
ous landing involving
British Empire and
French troops began on
26 April 1915. It was
Churchill's attempt at a
war of movement and a
link-up with Russia
through the Black Sea.
It was thwarted by stiff
Turkish resistance and
the Allies withdrew on
20 December. The
ANZACs (Australia New
Zealand Army Corps)
became a new national
legend in their countries.

The war at sea

The last moments of the German armoured cruiser *Blücher* after the skirmish on the Dogger Bank, January 1915. More than 700 of the ship's company were drowned. The main force of three German battle cruisers escaped, however.

Submarine offensive
A German torpedo hits a British freighter, 1916 (left).
In April 1917 Britain's ammunition and food reserves
were drastically reduced by submarine attacks. This was
remedied by the use of naval convoys. German sub-
marines scuttled by their crews at Scapa Flow in
Scotland in 1919, to avoid having to hand them over to
Britain under the peace terms agreed at
Versailles (above).

Peace to End All Peace

British and French staff officers stand on tables to look into the Hall of Mirrors where the peace treaty is being signed on 28 June 1919 at Versailles. A young British aide called it a 'peace to end all peace', its punitive measures against Germany a recipe for future vengeance.

THE PHONEY PEACE

Germany in Turmoil

The period from 1919 to 1939 is now seen by some historians a continuation of hostilities by other means, part of what General de Gaulle called 'the Thirty Years War of our century'. The 1918 armistice and peace talks triggered fighting within Germany, and across Europe. In January 1919 a group of Communist activists, the Spartacists, staged a rising in Berlin. They are seen driving through Berlin the previous month (right). Led by Rosa Luxemburg and Karl Liebknecht, they demanded a socialist republic modelled on the Bolshevik regime which had just taken over in Russia. The Spartacists were quickly defeated by government soldiers and the Socialist Peoples' Militia and right-wing Freikorps. Luxemburg and Liebknecht were arrested and subsequently murdered by their captors.

For Germany the terms of the peace were particularly harsh. The reparations demanded under the terms of the Versailles conference were condemned as short-sighted by some liberals like Lloyd George, who foresaw they would fuel further conflict. Under the terms French troops occupied the Ruhr and British troops followed to collect reparation debts. The German Fleet, interned at Scapa Flow, scuttled itself.

Germany suffered huge inflation, and the value of the mark halved in a fortnight in June 1923. In November extremists staged another coup, which quickly failed. This time it was a group from the right under Field Marshal von Ludendorff and an obscure ex-corporal, Adolf Hitler, leader of the Nazi or National Socialist Party. At Munich's biggest beer hall Hitler called for a national dictatorship but, after a demonstration by his 'brown shirt' supporters was dispersed by the police, he fled and was then captured and imprisoned. Who would then have guessed that eleven years later the Nazis would be able to mount a rally like this at Nuremberg (previous page)?

Street fighting 1919
Battles between the
Spartacists on one side
and the army, the rival
Socialist Militia and the
Freikorps on the other,
in Berlin, led to the
defeat of the
Communists and the
murder of their leaders
Rosa Luxemburg and
Karl Liebknecht
in January.

Munich Putsch
Weapons being distributed to National Socialist party members in Munich just before Hitler called for a coup in the beer hall on 8 November 1923.

Russia: Red and White

Weak government, food and fuel shortages and the terrible plight of the forces at the front led to riots in Petrograd in February and the abdication of Tsar Nicholas II. Desertions from the Army continued throughout the summer, but a Bolshevik coup failed in July. The Germans decided to help Lenin return and destroy Russia from within. In October he launched another coup with the help of 40,000 Red Guards, and the interim government of Kerensky surrendered. On 3 March 1918 the Bolsheviks signed the Treaty of Brest-Litovsk with Germany, and Russia recognised the independence of Ukraine, Georgia, Poland, Finland and the Baltic States. By then the new Bolshevik regime and Red Army were facing civil war from royalist officers under the leadership of Admiral Kolchak.

British, French and American troops were sent in March 1918 to support the White Russian forces, as the royalists were called, and 'protect' Allied interests in Murmansk and Archangel. From late 1918 the Ukraine was the scene of fierce fighting, as first the Bolsheviks and then the White Guard under General Denikin seized it and ruled it with great brutality – until defeated in 1920. By then Kolchak's forces had been driven east to Vladivostok. Japanese forces, part of the Allied intervention in Siberia, did not leave the eastern part of that area until 1922. The Red Army succeeded largely due to brilliant organisation of its forces by the Bolshevik Commissar for War, Leon Trotsky, though its members could be studiedly unmilitary in their bearing, like the Red Guard with stick grenades in his belt in 1919 (right). They were helped greatly by the incompetence of the White leadership. By 1920 much of southern and western Russia had been devastated – worse was to follow with the purges of the kulaks – wealthier peasants – and repeated famine, brought on by the economic policies of the Communists.

Arms training

Young factory workers look a little tentative in their
handling of their rifles in the Civil War (above).

July Massacre, Petrograd

An attempted Bolshevik coup against the 'Mensheviks'
(moderate Social Democrats) and Kerensky's interim
government failed in July 1916 (previous page). Here the
police shoot down the Bolsheviks in the street. This
month Lenin fled for his life to Finland.

Petrograd, winter 1917

Red Guards crouching in the snow. The formality of the
composition suggests that this is a propaganda shot.

Intervention

In March 1918 British, American and French troops
were sent in to support the Whites and 'guard Allied
interests'. Here American troops move into Vladivostok
in the Far East.

Uneasy peace
Germans arrive in Kiev, Ukraine, 1918, to take up polic-
ing duties in the country made independent after the
signing of the Treaty of Brest-Litovsk by Russia
and Germany.

Under the Kremlin walls

The fledgling Red Army parades in Moscow's newly-rechristened Red Square at a time when White loyalist armies were threatening from several directions.

Red cavalry

Soldiers of the First Cavalry Army, the largest concentration of disciplined cavalry ever, under the hammer-and-sickle banner in 1920, when they got within fifteen miles of Warsaw. Because their lines of communication were then so long, the Poles were able to turn them back. Note the signs of exhaustion on their faces.

Improvisation
Anti-aircraft machine gun mounted on a cart of the Red
1st Horse Cavalry Army, 1920.

Soldiers' burial

Burial of Red Guards, Vladivostok, 1918. Though the mourners wear full costume, there are no priests in sight, an indication of the new regime.

Struggle in Ireland

Rebellion had been festering in Ireland for centuries, and in 1916 it burst out into the open again with the Easter Rising. The Irish Republican Brotherhood, the military wing of the nationalist party Sinn Fein (Ourselves, Alone) seized the Post Office in O'Connell Street in Dublin, and declared an Irish Republic.

Fighting broke out in the centre of Dublin, until the leaders of the rebellion were rounded up and executed by firing squad. However, Sinn Fein won a large number of seats in the first post-war general election for the Westminster Parliament – known in Irish history as the Sinn Fein election. They did not take their seats. By this time a full-scale guerrilla insurgency was under way across Ireland. The British raised 400 reinforcements for the Royal Irish Constabulary. These 'Black and Tans' became a byword for undisciplined brutality. They were both augmented by a further 1,500 'Auxiliary' militia. Thanks to them the British Prime Minister Lloyd George boasted 'we have murder by the throat'. But by December 1921 the Anglo-Irish Treaty had signed away British rule in southern Ireland, though six Ulster counties in the north were exempted, because of their Protestant majorities, becoming the Northern Ireland of today.

The militants rejected the Treaty, as it gave Ireland the status of a Commonwealth Dominion, like Canada, and not full independence. The anti-Treaty men formed themselves into the Irish Republican Army, and fought a guerrilla war against the Free State forces, such as the sniper at a Dublin window in 1922 (right). This soon degenerated into a campaign of assassinations. The man who signed the Treaty, Michael Collins, was shot in an ambush. In the summer of 1923 the war came to an end, as the Free State government gained the upper hand.

Irish Civil War

Free State soldiers use a bus for a mobile roadblock at
Blessington, near Dublin, July 1922. It also keeps
them dry.

Irish Republican Army

Anti-Treaty men behind a barricade in Dublin, in July
1922, ignored by cyclists and pedestrians.

173

O'Connell Street

This had been bombarded by the Royal Navy during the
Easter Rising in 1916, and was further devastated in the
Civil War in July 1922.

The gunmen

The IRA in Grafton Street, Dublin during the fighting in
the capital in July 1922. The figure on the left is no
doubt holding a revolver inside his macintosh.

China: War and Invasion

Following the overthrow of the last Emperor in 1911, China was soon in a state of civil war. Sun Yat Sen's nationalist Kuomintang party struggled to maintain authority, and warlords ruled large tracts of the country. In 1923 Sun tried to forge an alliance with the Communists to defeat the warlords. But this came to an end with Sun's death in 1925 and the succession to the leadership of the Kuomintang of Chiang Kai-shek, who was violently anti-Communist. Sun's democratic and socialist ideals were soon forgotten and Chiang's dictatorship was cemented by his Kuomintang forces, typified by the soldier with his Mauser machine pistols in 1927 (right).

In 1934 the Communists decided the only way to survive was to march from Kiangsi in the south-west to the mountains of Yennan in northern Shensi, a distance of nearly 6,000 miles. The Long March took nearly a year. Nearly 100,000 of the 200,000 who set out became casualties. But it cemented Mao Tse Tung's leadership and the influence of his deputy Chou En-lai in the Communist Party. Eventually they would defeat Chiang Kai-shek in 1949.

In September 1931 Japan engineered the Mukden Incident – in which they claimed the Mukden - Port Arthur railway had been sabotaged – to sieze this key city – and the rest of Manchuria by the end of the year. The following year Manchuria was proclaimed the 'independent state of Manchukuo', under the puppet Emperor Henry Pu-yi, though Japan was in control.

In July 1937 Tokyo launched a full-scale invasion of northern China after it claimed that Japanese troops had been attacked at the Marco Polo Bridge near Beijing. Nanking, Shanghai and the eastern seaboard were seized after heavy fighting and hideous atrocities. In two years of fighting 800,000 Chinese troops were killed to about 40,000 Japanese. Chiang Kai-shek retreated to Chungking.

Kuomintang forces

Soldiers from the left wing of the Kuomintang army,
commanded by Chiang Kai-shek, parade in Hangkou in
1927, part of his successful 'Northern Expedition' that
reunified much of China. They retain their traditional
broad-brimmed 'coolie' straw hats. Foreigners mistook
these for shields, seeing them as symbols of the back-
ward state of Chinese forces. The standard-bearer has
an umbrella.

A Cantonese prisoner

He is brought in alive by his captors in 1927, though whether they are Communists, followers of a freelance warlord, or Kuomintang has been forgotten. The picture stands as a witness to the casual brutality prevalent in China for so many decades. .

International interests
Warships riding at anchor off the Bund, the esplanade at
Shanghai, 1927. They are standing by to assist their
communities in the event of rioting in this international-
ly controlled city. The first is a Japanese light cruiser,
followed by American, French and British ships.

Japanese attack Shanghai, 1932
After their coup in Manchuria the Japanese mounted an
invasion of the Chinese sections of Shanghai in 1932.
Chinese troops fought back and after three months a
face-saving settlement was reached. Japanese troops
halt whilst an observer up a ladder looks through his
binoculars at the Chinese positions (left). Japanese navy
gunners in Shanghai (above).

The rape of Nanking
A poignant scene at the railway station in Nanking during the Japanese invasion of northern China, November 1937. Between 200,000 and 300,000 civilians died in the onslaught on Nanking.

Bombed by mistake
The scene is the Cathay Hotel, one of the most famous in China, close to the Bund in Shanghai, in September 1937 after Chiang Kai-shek's planes dropped their bombs on the city, missing the Japanese warships at anchor off the Bund because of the high wind. British soldiers can be seen in the picture. The Japanese landed troops shortly after.

Italy in Abyssinia

The Italian dictator Benito Mussolini determined to expand his empire in Africa in the mid-thirties – and deliberately chose to reverse one of the biggest humiliations of his country in a previous era, the Italian army's defeat by Abyssinian troops at the battle of Adowa in 1896. Il Duce, as the Italian leader styled himself, in 1935 prepared to invade Abyssinia (today's Ethiopia) from Italy's colonies of Eritrea and Somalia. Part of the preparations was to get God on side, hence the blessing of the guidon of an Alpino Legionary unit while the portrait of Il Duce looked on (right). Deliberately ignoring the pleas of the League of Nations, the Italian army crossed into Abyssinia and headed towards Adowa on 3 October 1935.

In Addis Ababa, the Emperor Haile Selassie issued a call to arms. 'Arise, each one of you, take up arms to defend your Emperor and your country', the tribal elders were told by proclamation. But Adowa soon fell, though the Italian advance slowed down, and at the end of November General De Bono was replaced by General Badoglio. The Abyssinian forces, using their knowledge of the broken terrain and the capricious climate, successfully counterattacked in Tigre. The Italians then used mustard gas – still a matter of huge controversy in Italy. The following year Haile Selassie mounted a last stand at Mai Ceu, but was defeated. Badoglio took Addis Ababa on 5 May 1936, and General Graziani seized the Ogaden. Abyssinia was amalgamated with Eritrea and Somalia to form 'L'Africa Orientale Italiana' (Italian East Africa).

Haile Selassie fled into French Somaliland, and would be restored by the British Ethiopian Campaign of 1941. Mussolini's Abyssinia campaign provided material for several fine novels like Carlo Levi's *Christ Stopped at Eboli* and Evelyn Waugh's comic masterpiece on war reporting, *Scoop*.

Bombing up

Italian planes being loaded with bombs, Abyssinia 1935.
Later in the campaign the Italians used mustard gas
bombs, which brought condemnation from the League
of Nations – to little effect.

The Emperor rides out

An armed guard strides beside the Emperor Haile
Selassie (1891-1975), mounted on a mule as he goes to
inspect troops in the autumn of 1935.

Forces of the Emperor
An amazonian guerrilla warrior in Abyssinia 1935-36
(left). Abyssinian troops moving up to battle November
1935 (above). The troops of Haile Selassie were tem-
peramentally highly strung, but exceedingly brave in the
heat of battle. They managed to check the Italian forces
equipped with tanks and aircraft in Tigre in December
1935.

The Spanish Civil War

The Spanish Civil War's origins and much of the way in which it was fought are very Spanish, though German and Italian air and ground forces fought for Franco's Nationalists while left-wingers from around the world joined the Republican International Brigades. The victory in elections of a leftist Popular Front triggered a military coup by General Franco. The failure of this set off the civil war. The Nationalists had the better generals in Franco and Mola, and more coherent tactics and sense of political purpose. They also had much better munitions, artillery and planes than those supplied to the Republicans by Russia.

In the first major battle, in the Guadarrama hills, the Nationalist advance on Madrid was repulsed. Several set-piece sieges indicated what was to come in World War II: that the civilian population would be on the front line and among the prime victims, like this child pulled half-naked from the rubble after a bombing raid in Barcelona in February 1938 (right). Cordoba and Granada quickly fell to Franco, but the heaviest fighting was in the north, in the Basque country and for Navarre and round Madrid. A second thrust on the capital was halted, temporarily, by a small Soviet tank force.

The leftists in the north, depicted in Orwell's *Homage to Catalonia*, fought several bloody counter-strikes in Aragon, but with little success. The Republican coalition was too fragmented and poorly supplied, and suffered from a deliberate policy by Britain, America and France to keep out, whereas Franco had the active support of Mussolini and Hitler. By early 1939 resistance was exhausted and thousands went from Catalonia into exile in France.

Work of the Condor Legion
Santander in flames during the northern offensive in 1938. The Basque provinces had already fallen and now it was the turn of Castile's only port, on the Bay of Biscay.

Republican rifles

Women preparing to take up position in the Republican front line, August 1936 (left).

Republican troops besieging army cadets holding out in the Alcazar in Toledo, July 1936 (above). Famously, the attacking Nationalist commander outside the city declined to negotiate for his son, one of the cadets, and said he should die for his country.

The last of Spain

A woman among the hundreds of thousands of refugees
waiting to cross into France in January 1939 (above). By
now the Republican cause was all but lost – giving way
to 36 years of Franco's dictatorship.

Surrender

Nationalists round up Republicans who have been holding shallow trenches along a ridge on the Somosierra Front in August 1936. Surrender was often followed by summary execution – by both sides.

Troubled Palestine

I n 1917 the British Foreign Secretary Arthur Balfour wrote to Lord Rothschild expressing sympathy for the idea that a Jewish homeland should be established in Palestine, but 'that nothing shall be done which may prejudice civil and religious rights of existing non-Jewish communities in Palestine'. The contradiction inherent in the Balfour Declaration still has no clear resolution: making Arabs and Jews co-exist in the old Turkish province. In 1923 the League of Nations' formal mandate for British rule over Palestine was enacted.

In 1918 the population had been 553,000 Muslims, 70,000 Christians (mostly Arab) and 85,000 Jews. By 1936 the Jews had reached 400,000, about one third of the total population. It was in this year that the Arabs started the Rebellion which was to last until 1939. Security operations, like this British soldier keeping watch over the Old City of Jerusalem in 1938 (right), were supervised by two young British commanders, Bernard Montgomery and Harold Alexander. The Jewish community had formed the Haganah, an underground armed self-defence force, which had some 15,000 under arms initially. Then, in 1931 there had come the formation of the more violent and proactive Irgun Zvai Leumi, associated with Vladimir Jabotinsky's Revisionist Movement, which wanted a separate Jewish State in the whole of Palestine.

The White Paper of 1939 declared the Jews should have a separate national home within an independent Arab Palestine. The following year Abraham Stern founded the Lehi, better known as the Stern Gang, which murdered the British Minister of State, Lord Moyne, in Cairo in November 1944. British troops were often the targets of both Arab and Jewish nationalists. Many of the Irgun were executed by the British for their violent acts of terrorism.

Arab terror
Jewish settlers gather at
a house in Tel Aviv
which has been set on
fire by Palestinian mili-
tants at the beginning of
the Arab rebellion, in
September 1936.

Fighters in their own causes

Arab prisoners rounded up in the Old City of Jerusalem
during the Arab rebellion, 1938 (above). Most of the
Arab traders in the Old City went on strike, which went
on until 1939. A member of the Haganah defence force
standing guard in her kibbutz, July 1938 (right). Many
women were fighters on the front line. Later the
Haganah became the Israeli Defence Force which, based
on conscription, has a high proportion of women soldiers – though they are not allowed to the battle front.

Hitler's Path to War

On 30 January 1933 Adolf Hitler became Chancellor of Germany. A month later, the parliament building, the Reichstag, burnt down mysteriously, and this allowed the Nazi Party to declare an emergency, and call elections for a new parliament, which ultimately delivered absolute power. Despite their loud contempt for democratic institutions, the Nazis liked a cloak of legality. In March many Germans were as happy as this small boy in his mini-SS uniform and jack boots (right).

Hitler's plans were simple: social engineering to create a master race and master economy in Germany, and to overturn the humiliating terms and conditions, and loss of territory imposed by the Treaty of Versailles. In June 1934 he dealt with his main rival Ernst Rohm, leader of the SA storm troopers, in the 'Night of the Long Knives'.

Hitler's game of diplomatic bluff succeeded superbly. In 1936 his troops reclaimed the Rhineland, previously occupied by French forces. France and Britain raised little protest. In March 1938 Austria was taken into Hitler's new German empire in the 'Anschluss'; in September he pressed for absorption of the 'Sudetenland' Germans in Czechoslovakia. At Munich the British and French agreed, a deal the British prime minister Chamberlain hailed as bringing 'peace in our time'. Hitler's Nazism, and his whole political credo, was profoundly racist and anti-Semitic. Jews were hounded from office and restricted from the first days of Nazi power. On *Kristallnacht*, 9 November 1938, mobs were encouraged to attack Jewish shops and synagogues, and the same followed in Austria a few days later.

In March 1939 Hitler moved into Prague after the Slovaks had split from the Czechs. In August he concluded a non-aggression treaty with Stalin's Russia. But it was Britain, considered a natural ally by Hitler, and France, that would not back down over Poland, and on 3 September declared war.

Master of the Master Race

Hitler addresses a rally in 1933. He is in Party uniform, with Swastika arm band. When President Hindenburg died in 1934, Hitler was proclaimed 'Führer of the German Reich' and all soldiers had to take an oath of loyalty to him.

The Rhineland reoccupied

Troops march in, violating the Locarno Pact of 1920. It
was a huge gamble because the soldiers did not have
enough ammunition to put up a fight.

Swastikas and flowers

Garlands and jackboots – a familiar mix in the Third
Reich. Girls in the Rhineland give flowers to the
German cavalry.

Invasion
German motorised
troops entering Prague
in 1939. Many in the
crowd seem less than
pleased, if not disgusted,
at the arrival of their
new masters, and what
look like Nazi salutes at
first sight are in fact
clenched fists.

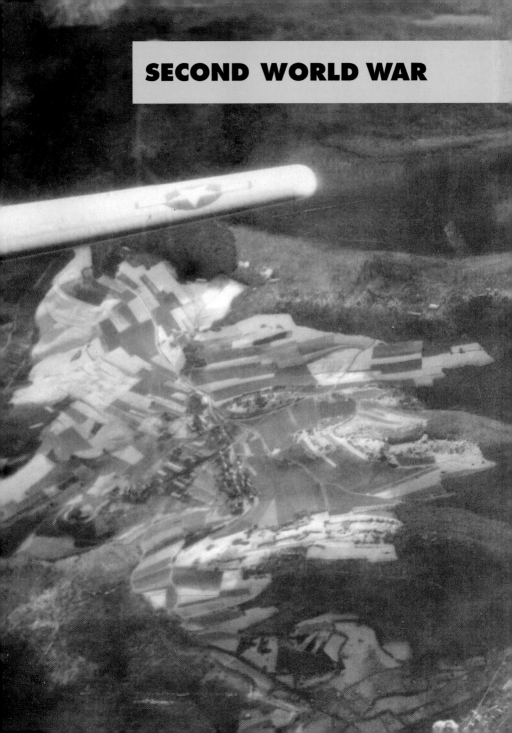

SECOND WORLD WAR

Poland fell in a month, partly because of Germany's air superiority, which was experienced by this father and daughter on a stretcher in a first aid station after Warsaw had been bombed on 17 September (right). Britain then failed to stop the fall of Norway. In May 1940 Hitler unleashed his air and ground forces in a Blitzkrieg strike through Holland and Belgium into France. By mid-June France sued for peace and the British had managed to scramble 330,000 troops, two-thirds British, away from the beaches of Dunkirk back to England. This escape from defeat was swiftly made into a moral victory.

Within weeks the Battle of Britain began in the air and was to endure until the end of October, when the Luftwaffe switched its main effort to night bombing. Britain had four assets; a superb plane in the Spitfire and a stalwart plane in the Hurricane; superb staffing by the RAF command under Hugh Dowding; radar and the mercurial and still unfathomable will and spirit of Winston Churchill. It was largely due to him that Britain would be the only power to be in the fight from 1939 to 1945.

On the battlefield, Hitler's legions rolled on. On 22 June 1941 three million men in 152 divisions were unleashed on Russia in Operation Barbarossa. By the summer of 1941 Erwin Rommel's Afrika Korps was galvanising Germany's Italian allies to chase the British out of Libya. By the autumn of 1941 it looked for a brief moment as if the Nazi New Order would rule Europe from the Atlantic to the Urals, but that was not allowing for new players entering the arena, like the USA, one of whose A-26 Invader bombers limps home over France, after its starboard engine has been set ablaze by enemy anti-aircraft fire (previous spread).

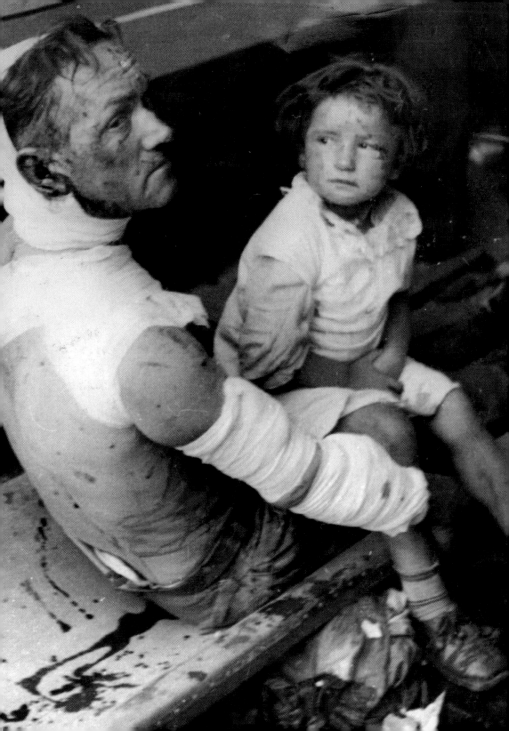

Poland invaded, September 1939

A woman tends a victim of Nazi atrocities in
Poland, 1939.

Warsaw outskirts
The Germans halted outside the Polish capital on
September 8 and then pounded it for a fortnight. The
government fled at the end of the month.

The Winter War

Finnish ski troops deployed in their war against Russia,
1939-40. The Finns put up stiff resistance, but in the
end had to cede territory to Russia. Ironically, British
troops were nearly sent to the aid of the Finns, since
Russia was at that stage allied to Germany.

Victim in the snow
A Russian frozen to death. The Finns later contributed
17 divisions to Hitler's attack on Russia in June 1941.
The Finns proved masters of Arctic warfare and taught
the Russians lessons in 1939-40 which they would put
to good use in the fighting across the Steppe against
Hitler's armies.

Blitzkrieg, France 1940
German storm troopers moving at the double through a
village in France in 1940, shielding their faces from the
heat of the flaming building.

Observation post
French artillery spotters in the top of a barn close to
their defensive Maginot Line, April 1940, before the
launch of the Blitzkrieg.

Heavy artillery

A German heavy howitzer firing from its mounting on a
train, France 1940. The soldier in the foreground has
just pulled the long lanyard attached to the
firing mechanism.

Moments of defeat, 1940
German soldiers watch the Dutch port of Rotterdam. It
was seized with the help of paratroops and seaplanes
landing on the river (above). A French Char B1 tank
crew member surrenders after his column has been halted by German motorised infantry in their sweep
through northern France in May 1940 (right).

Bombs and Doodlebugs

Firemen putting out fires after a daylight raid on the heart of the City in May 1941. The dome of St Paul's is unscathed in the background (above). A little girl is rescued after her home has been hit by a V-1 'Doodlebug' flying bomb, 20 June 1944 (right). The V-1 was to kill some 6,500 people in south-east England.

Rescue at Dunkirk
Altogether 338,000
troops were taken off
the beaches at Dunkirk
in a week, between
26 May and 4 June
1940. Craft of all sizes
sailed from Britain and
altogether 200 boats and
ships were lost, includ-
ing warships, as the RAF
could not maintain air
superiority over the
beaches. Crew of the
French destroyer
Bourrasque are hauled in
after their life raft sinks
(left). The *Bourrasque*
sinking after hitting a
mine (above right).
British troops firing at
aircraft, as they wait on
the beaches (right).

Germans in Paris

Officers relax outside a café in 1941, including members of the SS, on the right and in the centre background. A spell of leave in Paris was a much sought-after perk.

Arc de Triomphe
German horse-drawn artillery parade past this monument
to French military glory, after the fall of France in 1940.
An echo of the scene in March 1871 on pp. 48-49.

Yugoslavia, 1941
One of many villages (above) destroyed by the Nazis in
their take-over of the country so as to maintain supply
lines to the Afrika Korps in Libya. A German officer
taps out a propaganda despatch on the devastated outskirts of Belgrade (right).

Round-up Warsaw

Jews from the Ghetto surrender after their unsuccessful
uprising, in 1943. In 1940 300,000 Jews were trapped
in the Ghetto. In June 1943 60,000 surrendered there.

Firing squad

Polish civilians are shot. This photograph was smuggled to the United States through the Polish underground. In 1943 the mass grave of 4,000 Polish officers was discovered in Katyn Wood. They had been executed in 1939 by the Russians who had shared the dismemberment of Poland with the Germans.

Desert Rats

British infantry capture the crew of a German Tiger
Tank in the Western Desert, as the tide begins to turn at
El Alamein in 1942. They are from the 8th Army, the
Desert Rats.

Desert Fox

General Erwin Rommel observing the battle for Tobruk.
A charismatic figure and brilliant tank commander, he
was admired as much by his foes as his friends.

Western leaders
(right to left) Winston Churchill, General Charles de
Gaulle, President Franklin Roosevelt and French general
Henri Giraud at the Casablanca Conference in French
Morocco, January 1943 (above). They were there to
decide on the next phase of the Mediterranean war, and
Sicily rather than Sardinia was chosen as the target. The
Conference also helped de Gaulle to establish himself
further as leader of the Free French, as can be detected
from the body language of himself and his rival Giraud.

Into Sicily
Canadian troops street fighting in 1943(right). The
British VIIIth Army had a tougher time here than the
Americans under General George Patton. They were
held up at Catania and Churchill was warned that many
British infantry units were wary of fighting over
open ground.

Sicily, Italy

Shot-up road signs and a perforated Duce in Messina as
American and British forces liberate Sicily (left). General
Kesselring and General Guzzoni carried out a wily
retreat and managed to get nearly 100,000 troops
across the Straits of Messina to fight on the Italian
mainland. German soldiers surrender to Americans in
Cisterna 1944 (above) after the Allies had landed at
Anzio, sixty miles behind the German front. It would
take another year to defeat Kesselring's forces.

War in Russia

Stalin was caught largely unprepared in June 1941, having ignored clear indications from intelligence that Germany was preparing a massive invasion. Hundreds of thousands of Russian troops were surrounded and the Germans believed that Leningrad and Moscow would soon be in their grasp. With the help of the onset of the cruel Russian winter, for which the Germans weren't equipped, and of troops rapidly transferred from far-eastern Siberia, the Russian generals held the line. They then organised the forces for the long strike back, the Great Patriotic War, which was to cost Russia somewhere in the region of 20 million dead. In this they were helped by partisans, like these two in a corn stack (right).

In the late summer of 1942 von Paulus' Sixth Army headed for Stalingrad hoping, once it had been taken, to secure the Caucasus oilfields round Baku. The city was reduced to rubble, which provided natural obstacles, that could be fiercely defended by General Chuikov. General Zhukov then planned a pincer round von Paulus and his supporting forces in late November. After a huge encircling battle in driving snow and fog, von Paulus surrendered with some 100,000 prisoners – 140,000 Germans and Romanians had already died in the battle. This was the war's turning point.

The Russians then fought huge armoured battles, the most decisive round Kursk, between 3 and 25 July 1943, the biggest tank battle in history. Though the Russians took more casualties, Kursk was a victory for them and Kiev, the capital of Ukraine was soon retaken.

The German commander Heinz Guderian fought a series of brilliant retreat actions, using the 'left hook counter-strike' which was later to be the key Nato ground tactic for more than 40 years. In 1944 Warsaw and Prague were liberated, and the Russians were on their way to Berlin.

Barbarossa

A German motorised infantry unit advances into the Ukraine, during Operation Barbarossa, June 1941. Kiev, the capital, fell within days.

The brutality of war

A boy hides his eyes as his house burns in Belorussia in1941 (above). A wounded Russian officer tries to direct the fire of his troops during the retreat battle in the summer of 1941 (right).

Time out

German troops pause
for refreshment in the
town of Vitebsk, emp-
tied and torched before
their arrival during the
advance in the summer
of 1941.

Reinforcements

Fresh troops, some just arrived from the far east of
Siberia, parade in snow-covered Red Square in Moscow,
November 1941, before being immediately thrown into
the defence of the city. The snow heralds the arrival of
'General Winter', Russia's best ally (above).

Murder

A woman is held by her husband after she finds the
body of her murdered son at Kerch in the Ukraine (left).

Stalingrad

Russian troops attacking across open ground. By this
time the Russian defenders were reduced to a front only
1500 metres deep on the west bank of the Volga. The
wrecked buildings, however, made excellent defences.
An epic picture by Georgi Zelma.

The fallen

Two iconic photographs, famous within Russia. The one
above celebrates the T-34, probably the best tank of the
war, as it charges past a German soldier, dead in the
snow. On the right "Ivan", the red Army infantryman,
charges as one of his squad is hit.

Kaput!
A German gunner holds
his head in his hands
and waits to surrender
after his field howitzer
has been knocked out. A
member of his gun team
lies dead beside him.
This was taken after the
Russians decisive victory
at Kursk (July 1943),
and repeatedly used by
the Red Army in its
propaganda.

By Air and Sea

For Britain after the surrender of France, the sea lanes became more than ever a lifeline. From 1939 to 1945 Britain faced a major submarine campaign from the German U-Boat fleet, known as the Battle of the Atlantic. Britain replied in kind, sending her submarines into the Mediterranean, where they suffered appalling casualties and nearly 50 per cent losses, and later to the Pacific.

In two hours, in a surprise attack on 7 December 1941, Yamamoto's torpedo bombers sunk or destroyed most of the US Pacific Fleet in Pearl Harbor, including the battleship *Arizona* with 1,100 of her crew (right). Admiral Yamamoto was not satisfied. The American aircraft carriers had not been in Pearl Harbor. 'We have woken a sleeping giant', he is alleged to have remarked, for he knew that America would win on industrial muscle alone. Altogether America would build 90 aircraft carriers during the war – and the British would build or plan some 50.

The carriers brought a new dimension to naval warfare; great battle fleets would engage without ever sighting each other. Lack of air cover lost Britain two capital ships, the *Prince of Wales* and the *Repulse*, to Japanese planes off Singapore at the end of 1941. Great carrier battles were fought in the Coral Sea and at Midway in 1942.

Over Europe thousand of bomber-raids were flown by RAF Bomber Command on Hamburg and Berlin. The US Strategic Air Command, and the 8th Tactical Air Force steadily commanded the skies from the D-Day landings in June 1944. In February 1945 British bombers hit Dresden and more than 60,000 civilians died in the firestorm.

The Japanese and the Germans managed to fight on, with very little air power at all. The Japanese used Kamikaze suicide bombers to devastating effect against the American and British fleets.

Pearl Harbor
Ground crew look on
after an attack by
Japanese Zero and Val
bombers at Ford Island.
The air bases at
Hickham and Wheeler
were also pummelled. In
the harbour the USS
Shaw explodes.

Battle of the Coral Sea

The Japanese carrier group came across the American carriers *Lexington* and *Yorktown* as the group moved in to take Port Moresby in New Guinea, 7-8 May 1942. The Americans sank one escort carrier and badly damaged another carrier, so that the Japanese turned back. The *Lexington* was damaged, but still able to steam. However, a later internal explosion meant that she had to be sunk. Here the crew of the *Lexington* prepare to abandon ship as a rescue vessel stands off to pick up survivors.

Kamikaze

A dramatic picture of a Japanese suicide fighter packed
with explosives as it is about to hit a US capital ship in
1945 (above). The gun crew seem quite unaware of
what is about to happen. Kamikaze means 'divine wind'
and became a cult for young pilots who saw themselves
as privileged to die for their emperor. Deck crew run
from an exploding Kamikaze (right). US carriers were
vulnerable because they had wooden decks – British carrier decks were made of steel.

Engage, Engage!
Anti-aircraft pom pom guns in action on the US aircraft
carrier *Hornet* off Japan, February 1945, while its planes
bomb Tokyo. Note the fire controller and some of the
crew do not wear helmets. Later all crew would wear
anti-flash balaclavas and gloves.

Final run

A Japanese 'Jill' torpedo bomber levels to the deck for the final attacking run, Pacific, 1945.

Last moments
A boat pulls away from the stricken British destroyer
HMS *Kelly*, commanded by Lord Louis Mountbatten,
off Crete, 1941.

Going down

German U-boat crew observe the last moments of their victim, an American freighter, in the Battle of the Atlantic.

Flying Fortress

The Flying Fortress B-17
was the backbone of the
Allied daytime bombing
offensive on Germany. It
had greater ability to
defend itself than the
RAF's Avro Lancaster,
including a waist gunner
who could fire back at
fighters attacking from
below. A spectacular
shot of attacking B-17s
in formation with
vapour trails.

Air attack

A B-24 Liberator flying low over the oil refineries at
Ploesi in Romania after dropping its bomb load, proba-
bly incendiaries (left). The nose gunner's view, in a
Messerschmitt 110, of what looks like a dog fight over
Britain in 1941 (above).

The Pacific and Asia

'I will return' was the boast of General Douglas MacArthur when he was evicted by the Japanese from the Philippines in 1942. MacArthur's stratagem was 'island hopping,' moving from island group to island group, missing out some in between, like the island of Rabaul, and leaving the Japanese garrisons there to be starved of supplies. The troops coming ashore from the tank landing craft (right) are landing on one of the Marshall Islands in April 1944.

MacArthur disputed Nimitz's claim that the Philippines had no strategic significance, and insisted on honouring his pledge by returning there in 1944. The Japanese fleet tried to mount an ambush on the landings at Leyte Gulf – which very nearly succeeded. As it turned out, the US navy effectively eliminated the Japanese fleet as a fighting force there, one of the most decisive naval battles of the entire war.

The two last island battles, Iwo Jima and Okinawa, proved the most costly. At Iwo Jima the Japanese had turned the whole island into a fortress. The US marines sustained 26,000 casualties in four weeks. The Japanese pledged to die fighting, which 99 per cent of them did. At Okinawa in June 1945 the Japanese pursued the same tactics, and, it is said, persuaded President Harry S Truman that it would be necessary to drop the atomic bombs to end the war.

Two other land campaigns were pursued against the Japanese in mainland Asia. US General 'Vinegar Joe' Stilwell galvanised three Chinese divisions and Orde Wingate's 'Chindits' into rearguard action against the Japanese in Burma and China. More remarkable was the work of General 'Uncle Bill' Slim and his 14th Army. His Burma campaign was one of the hardest fought of the war, with decisive set piece battles at Arakan, Imphal and Kohima.

Beach assault
US Marines at the ready to fight their way inland after
an amphibious landing. They are under fire from the
jungle, Pacific Islands, 1944.

Jungle warfare
US marines prepare to set out on a jungle patrol on
Bougainville Island in the Solomons, 1944.

A rare sight

Japanese prisoners of war being brought in at
Guadalcanal, February 1943. They have been starved of
supplies and are emaciated. Most Japanese soldiers
fought to the death. When the Japanese finally retreated from the island in this month it gave the Americans
their first base in the Solomons. US marines had first
landed there in August 1942.

Street fighting

Japanese troops at the double as they fight to secure
Ichang during their seizure of Hupei Province, mainland
China, 1943.

Americans and Chinese

An American-trained Chinese machinegunner fights at
Changteh, which changed hands four times in 40 days,
before Japan's eventual defeat in China. US Forces in
China were commanded by Lt Gen 'Vinegar Joe'
Stilwell, who violently disagreed with his British
Supreme Allied Commander, Admiral Lord Louis
Mountbatten.

The advance to Rangoon

General Slim's 14th Army seized Rangoon on 2 May
1945, after a daring pursuit battle to beat the onset of
the monsoon. Here Lance Corporal T. Watson of the
Border Regiment brings in a Japanese prisoner at Pegu,
a vital junction in the advance to Rangoon. The
Borderers in Burma are described in George
MacDonald Fraser's *Quartered Safe Out Here*, the best
soldier's account of a British campaign in the Second
World War.

End Game

The landings in Normandy on the 6 June 1944 spelt the beginning of the end for the German forces in Western Europe. Two days earlier American and British forces had entered Rome. The fight would still be hard and bitter. The battle in Normandy did not go smoothly, with disagreements between British and American commanders which led to an inability to break out quickly round Caen. In Italy the Allies made equally heavy weather as their forces were depleted for use on other fronts and they were fighting through a full-blown Italian civil war.

Commanders like Rommel knew that with the Allies back in Western Europe Hitler could not win the war. In July a group of officers, with Rommel's tacit blessing, tried to blow Hitler up. The bomb was placed by Count von Stauffenberg, but Hitler moved at the last moment and was only wounded.

Increasingly Hitler was living in his own dream world. But his forces were still capable of effective counter strikes. In the Ardennes at the end of the year they hit back in 'the Battle of the Bulge', when Panzer forces nearly broke through the American lines. Montgomery was quickly despatched to help out General Omar Bradley.

But the heaviest fighting was in the east as the Russians threw huge armies across Europe and the Germans called up the over-fifties and boys, like this fifteen-year-old captured by the US 9th Army in April (right). The battle for Berlin itself was one of the bloodiest. But on 30 April Hitler committed suicide and the city surrendered on 2 May. Fighting continued in the Pacific for three months until atomic bombs had been dropped on Hiroshima on 7 August, and on Nagasaki on 9 August.

The wade ashore
US troops landing on
D-Day 6 June. Those
nearer the shore are
under German machine
gun fire.

D-Day Plus 2

American troops start making roadways from the
'Mulberry' harbour being built out at sea, 8 June 1944.
The quantity of shipping gives an idea of the scale and
complexity of the operation.

Air assault
An Allied airborne landing near the beachhead between Marseilles and Nice in the south of France, August 1944. Earlier, landings by the 1st and 82nd US Airborne divisions in the west and the British 6th Airborne Division in the east secure the flanks for the main D-Day amphibious landing. This photograph shows the sort of density which paratroopers hoped to achieve in the dropping zone.

Defence of Cologne

An Allied tank has been hit and its crew run for cover during the battle for Cologne 7 March 1945. Cologne Cathedral can be seen in the background.

Snipers in Paris

Crowds dive for cover at Notre Dame after snipers
open fire. Paris has just been liberated and is welcoming
General de Gaulle, August 1944. The ciné-cameraman
tries to capture the action.

Italian amazons

Partisans from the Partito d'Azione, Milan 1945. Milan,
like Genoa, was liberated by the partisans – who here,
manage to maintain surprising poise and 'bella figura' –
well before the Allies could get there.

Prisoners and collaborators

German prisoners, part of the Paris garrison, tend each other's wounds after their surrender, August 1944 (above). A group of Parisian women accused of being German collaborators, stripped and shaved as a public humiliation (right).

Driving home the attack

Russian troops charge down a street in Poland in 1944 during the Red Army advance westward through Europe.

Defeat
Exhausted Germans sleep during the battle in France
in 1944.

Victory

Allies' handshake. US GIs of 271st Regiment shake
hands with Russian soldiers on a bridge over the Elbe at
Torgau, 27 April 1945.

Destruction and exile
Women and children flee from bombardment in a
German town, April 1945.

Ashes of Dresden
The results of a devastating bombing raid in February
1945 by 800 bombers of the RAF which caused a huge
fire storm killing at least 60,000 civilians, and possibly
many more, raising doubts about the justification for
strategic bombing.

Symbolic moment

Red Army tommy-gunners putting up the Red Flag on
the roof of the Reichstag in Berlin on 30 April 1949,
though fighting continues inside the building. The next
day Marshal Chuikov will order his artillery to bombard
it. This was in fact a recreated scene because the original
hoisting of the flag took place when it was too dark
to photograph.

COLD WAR AND CONFLICT

Iron Curtain

The Cold War between the West and the USSR began almost before Winston Churchill declared at Fulton, Missouri that 'an iron curtain has descended across the Continent', on 5 March 1946. One of its first manifestations was the war being fought against the Communists in Greece. Stalin's old paranoia and grip on power was manifest in heavy purges at home and the imposition of Communist regimes in Eastern Europe, most notably in Prague, Warsaw, East Berlin, and Budapest.

In Europe the first direct confrontation was the passive siege of West Berlin, circumvented by the Berlin Airlift, starting in June 1948. At its height the Allies flew in 5,500 tonnes of supplies a day.

Frustrated dissidents rose against Communist rule throughout the fifties and sixties, in Berlin and Poland, most notably in Hungary in 1956, and in the Prague Spring of 1968. In 1961 the Communists in East Germany built a wall across Berlin to stop the leakage of dissidents to the West. It was damaged by a bomb in 1962, but the East Germans were quick to mend it (right).

The following year, the superpowers faced the reality of nuclear war in the Cuban Crisis – when the US discovered Russia was preparing missile sites on Cuba for weapons that could strike cities across America. President Kennedy forced Nikita Khrushchev to back down and take his technicians out of Cuba.

By 1964 another confrontation between the US and Communism was developing in Vietnam with the Americans beginning by helping to keep South Vietnamese forces supplied (previous page). The war would run until 1975 – leaving a legacy of recrimination and of mythology still potent today.

It was the fall of the Berlin Wall, in November 1989, that signalled the collapse of Communism in eastern Europe and the end of the Cold War.

Front line Berlin

A US Air Force C-54 Skymaster bringing supplies to
Berlin during the airlift in 1948 (above). Skymasters and
Dakotas were the workhorses of the huge lift, which carried coal as well as food. East German soldiers on a T-34
tank watch the frontier between the east and west zones
in Berlin, 1963 (left).

Hungarian revolution
Soviet tanks in central Budapest, 5 November 1956. The
Soviets crushed the rebellion while the world was distract-
ed by the Suez Crisis.

Tables turned

A Hungarian secret policeman is marched off by two
rebelling citizens of Budapest in 1956.

Prague Spring

A demonstration in Prague against the arrival of Soviet
armoured columns about to put down the 'Prague
Spring', led by Alexander Dubcek, 1968.

Molotov cocktail

A primitive petrol bomb is thrown at a Soviet tank in
Prague, 25 August 1968. Many Czech dissidents fled to
asylum in the West. Some like Vaclav Havel, the play-
wright and future President, stuck it out under the new
Soviet crackdown.

Civil war in Greece

The Russians backed the Communist EAM-ELAS insurgents. First Britain and then America backed the Monarchists, who won thanks to US airpower. Here an exhausted ELA guerrilla surrenders in Ipiros.

Communist prisoners

In Thessaloniki in 1947, the signs on their chests spell out
in French 'Britain must go'.

Malaya, Korea, Indo-China

The Communist Malayan Races' Liberation Army, almost exclusively ethnic Chinese in make-up, assassinated the British High Commissioner Sir Henry Gurney in 1952. He was replaced by General Sir Gerald Templer who directed a long counter-insurgency campaign, revolutionising training in jungle warfare and anti-guerrilla tactics. One of his weapons was the Special Air Service, reconstituted in 1948 to fight in Malaya. SAS soldiers are seen rescuing a colleague in the jungle (right). The rebels were cut off from their bases in the jungle, and from their supply lines through the 'squatter' camps of the ethnic Chinese community.

The Korean War blew up in 1950 as Stalin and his new ally, Mao, who had finally seized power over all China from Chiang Kai-shek's Kuomintang, decided that the American grip on the southern part of the Korean Peninsula was unsure. They backed the bid by the leader of the Communist North, Kim il Sung, to unite the country under his rule. In late June 1950 the North Korean Army invaded, and soon pushed the southern forces and their American allies right down the peninsula to Pusan.

In September the Americans and Commonwealth allies, fighting under the flag of the new United Nations, executed a daring amphibious operation at Inchon and pushed into the North. China then came into the war. The US commander, Douglas MacArthur, argued that nuclear weapons should be used – and President Truman sacked him. Fighting was extraordinarily bitter as 'human waves' of Chinese troops were thrown in. At one point British troops sprayed their own tanks with machinegun fire to hit Chinese climbing on them. The war ground to stalemate on the 38th Parallel in 1953, where the division between north and south still is.

Korea, and France's failure to re-establish control of Indo-China in 1954, should have been a warning of what might come a decade later in Vietnam.

Justice out East

A Communist soldier shoots a Chinese landowner in the
year the Communists take power in China, 1949 (above).
Alleged 'Communist sympathisers' being taken off to be
shot by the South Korean police, Pusan 1950 (right). This
photograph was taken by Bert Hardy and the suppression
of his story by the proprietors of *Picture Post* magazine,
the UK's principal photojournalism paper, triggered its
decline and demise.

Korean devastation

A GI patrolling the port area of Inchon after American
and Allied troops had seized it from the sea in a tricky
amphibious landing operation in September 1950 (left).
The aftermath of an air raid on the North Korean capital
of Pyongyang as the Americans seized it in October
1950 (above).

Air drop
French soldiers watching reinforcements dropping in by parachute to the besieged fortress of Dien Bien Phu, Indo-China (Vietnam), 1954. The outpost fell that summer, which meant the end of French rule, and Vietnam was divided, with the Communists under Ho Chi Minh ruling the north from Hanoi.

Vietnam and Cambodia

Vietnam was divided in two along the 17th Parallel when the French left in 1954. Within a few years the Communists in the north were reinforcing their supporters in the south. By 1961 the Kennedy administration in the US was becoming alarmed that a Communist takeover of the south was imminent. An incident in which a US warship, the *Maddox*, was fired on by North Vietnamese torpedo boats in August 1964 provoked a huge escalation of US military operations in Vietnam. Eventually more than half a million US personnel were engaged in the war, such as these US Marines assaulting a hill in 1966 (right).

The turning point was the offensive mounted by the North Vietnamese in the Chinese New Year, Tet, in 1968, in which they hoped to provoke a mass uprising throughout the south. That failed, and the Communists were defeated in the field, though they carried out a sustained battle for the fort at Khe Sanh and in the ancient capital Hue; they also managed to penetrate the outskirts of Saigon. At Khe Sanh massive airpower helped 7,000 US marines hold out against 40,000 North Vietnamese.

Tet was a political victory for the North, however, and American tried to disengage. But somehow the fight kept spreading, eventually into Cambodia and Laos. There were huge popular protests in the United States, culminating in the shooting dead of students by National Guardsmen at Kent State University in 1970. By 1971 the policy of 'Vietnamisation' had begun – handing over to the South Vietnamese Army.

When the next big push from the North came in 1975, there was no American air power to aid the south, and Saigon fell quickly at the end of April. In the same month the capital of Cambodia, Phnom Penh, fell to the Communists of the Khmer Rouge, who soon set up their 'killing fields', one of the most hideous episodes of the Cold War.

Hill Timothy, Vietnam
A picture by the legendary Larry Burrows of a light field gun being dropped in to Hill Timothy during the Tet Offensive, 1968.

Tables turned

A young girl guards a downed US pilot in the Vietnamese
jungle, October 1967.

At gunpoint
A Vietnamese peasant woman being held by a soldier
armed with a US M-16 carbine, 1969.

Air war, ground war
A US Air Force plane spraying Agent Orange defoliant to
strip the jungle and expose the Ho Chi Minh supply trail,
1966 (above). The spray caused huge damage to the environment and humans, but the supplies kept coming to the
Vietcong from the north. Vietcong fighting in the Quang
Tri-Thua area, South Vietnam, 1973 (right). The man on
the right is about to throw a grenade.

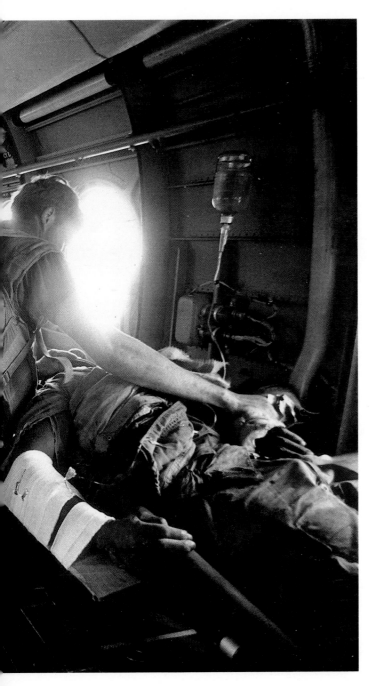

Medivac
A blood transfusion is given to a wounded soldier aboard a US Medivac helicopter in the Tet Offensive, February 1968. Picture by Terry Fincher.

A place of skulls, Cambodia

A heap of skulls discovered in 1980 at the site of one of the Khmer Rouge extermination camps at Tuoi Sleng. Under their ideologue commander Pol Pot, the Khmer Rouge implemented their plan for 'Year Zero', which entailed the murder or death by maltreatment of 2.5 million Cambodians in two years. Pol Pot was overthrown by a Vietnamese invasion in January 1979, and died under house arrest in 1998.

War in Latin America

The Cold War was fought out by proxy in Latin America, though the urban and rural civil wars there also had a dynamic of their own. Throughout the fifties the USA was accused of economic and cultural imperialism. One of the most successful revolutions against American interests was the seizure of power in 1959 in Cuba by Fidel Castro's Marxist revolutionary movement. One of his lieutenants was an Argentinian doctor, Ernesto 'Che' Guevara, destined to be the icon of the age of protest in the sixties (right). As a revolutionary commander he was something of a failure: captured by Bolivian troops in 1967 and shot dead.

In 1970 another Marxist, Salvador Allende was narrowly elected president of Chile, which he tried to turn into a fully-fledged socialist state. The armed forces aided by the CIA staged a coup in 1973, in which Allende died defending the presidential palace. General Pinochet took over and imposed a harsh regime.

In Central America civil wars erupted in El Salvador and Nicaragua, with lasting effects throughout the region. The US became embroiled in the Dominican Republic, eventually guaranteeing its autonomy in 1967, and Panama. Several military dictatorships faced challenges from urban and rural guerrilla movements such as the Montaneros in Argentina and the Tupamaros in Uruguay. In a desperate move to save itself the failing military dictatorship of Leopoldo Galtieri in Argentina ordered the invasion of the British colony of the Falkland Islands, which they claimed as theirs , in April 1982. This led to one of the strangest wars of the era.The British sent a Task Force 8,000 miles into the South Atlantic and recaptured the Islands in a land campaign lasting three weeks. The British lost four warships, with many damaged, and 255 men. The Argentines lost the cruiser *Belgrano* and 750 dead. The defeat brought the collapse of the Junta and the restoration of democracy.

El Salvador

In 1980 the Cardinal Archbishop of San Salvador, Oscar Romero, a champion of human rights, was assassinated by right-wing gunmen, at the Cathedral in San Salvador (above). In two years between 1979 and 1981 30,000 people were murdered by right-wing death squads. A Salvadoran soldier runs for cover during a fire fight with FMLN Marxist guerrilla in 1989 (left). Rebel attacks intensified that year because President Cristiani, of the American backed ARENA, was claimed to have rigged the elections.

Dominican Republic
US Marines entering a
house, some of the
30,000 landed on the
island to restore order
after ex-President Bosch,
previously overthrown in
a coup, tried to stage a
counter-coup in 1965.
The US repeated the
same kind of intervention
in Grenada in 1983, a
year after the
Falklands conflict.

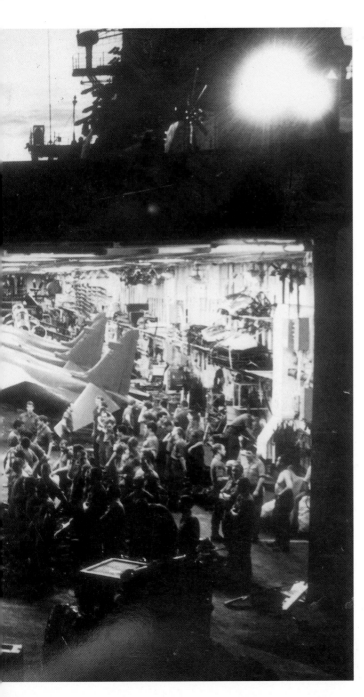

Dawn, South Atlantic
Air and ground crews of
the Sea Harriers together
with Royal Marines mus-
tered aboard the ageing
carrier HMS *Hermes*.
The British used their
limited airpower – about
30 to 40 Sea and Ground
Attack Harriers – with
great success, thanks
largely to the US AIM 9L
air-to-air missile. A
superb shot at dawn
action stations by
Martin Cleaver.

HMS *Antelope*
A Type 21 frigate, she
had been hit by bombs
while on escort duty on
26 May 1982. The crew
got off safely, but a bomb
'cooked', exploded later,
killing an ordnance dis-
posal officer and taking
the arm off another.
Here she is sinking in San
Carlos Water.

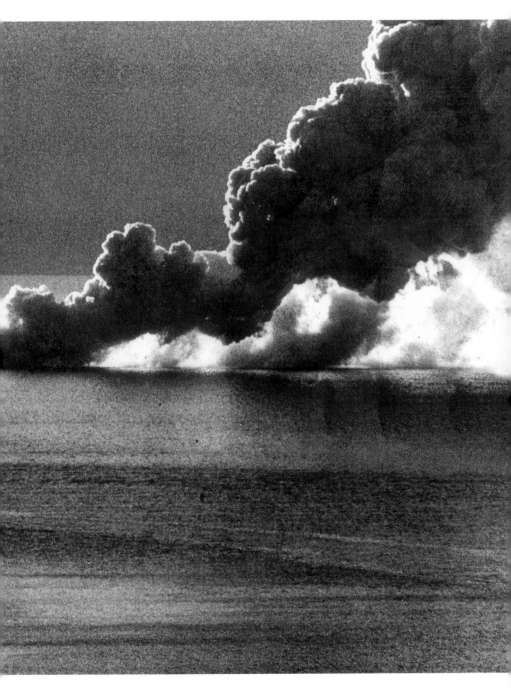

Falklands War

First Aid men with a badly burned member of the crew of
the destroyer HMS *Sheffield*, hit by an Exocet missile,
May 1982 (above). Argentine weapons being dumped
after the surrender,14 June 1982 (right).

Asian Divides

India and Pakistan were born out of British India in 1947 amid scenes of bloodshed. The neighbours were to go to war on three occasions, and the dispute over Kashmir is a running sore. It triggered a stalemate war in 1965. Both sides knew each other's tactics and training well – for both were products of British military training. In 1971 they fought over the claims of East Pakistan to independence. At least a million of its people were killed and ten million fled into India. The independent state of Bangladesh was born in 1972 – one of the poorest nations on earth.

In 1976 there was a rebellion of Tamil militants claiming their own home-land – 'Eelam' on the Jaffna Peninsula in Sri Lanka. After a ceasefire in 1987, 7,000 Indian peacekeeping troops were sent to Jaffna – but the fighting soon resumed. The Tamil Tiger fighters have proved adept as guerrillas, as the face of this apprehensive Sri Lankan soldier testifies (right).

Pakistan's precarious stability has been threatened by the upheavals in Afghanistan. She has twice reverted to military rule in recent years, under Zia ul-Haq and from 1999 under General Parvez Musharraf. In 1998 tension was heightened by both India and Pakistan holding underground nuclear weapons tests.

In 1973 King Zahir Shah of Afghanistan was overthrown by his prime minister General Daud Khan. Daud was murdered in 1978, and the follow-ing year Russia invaded to support their puppets, first Barbrak Kamal and then Dr Najibullah. The Russian troops were ambushed and harried by Mujahideen fighters aided by the West.

The Russians withdrew in 1989, and the Mujahideen entered Kabul in 1992 – though this did not bring peace. They were ousted in turn by the purist Taliban in 1996, who invited the Saudi renegade Osama bin Laden to base himself in Afghanistan.

Atrocities
'Traitors' being bayoneted to death by Mukti Bahini,
Indian extremists, during the war in 1971 which led to
the creation of Bangladesh (right). Pictures like this creat-
ed huge controversy among the photographers – some
witnessing such scenes refused to get their cameras out at
all, as they said it encouraged further atrocities. Men
accused of collaborating (above) with the Pakistanis wait
to be shot in Dacca by the Bangladeshis .

Afghan fighter-farmer

An Afghan guerrilla in the Mujahideen struggle against Russian occupation 1979-1989, amidst a field of the poppies which were to make Afghanistan one of the biggest opium producers in the world.

Jubilant Mujahideen

Guerrilla fighters on top of a Russian armoured personnel carrier which they have just captured (left). The Mujahideen proved adept at hit-and-run raids under darkness, though their military skills were quite primitive. A Russian convoy moves north up the Salang Highway through the Hindu Kush in the last retreat from Kabul in February 1989 (above). Gorbachev's decision to quit Afghanistan was a sure sign that his regime in Moscow was in trouble.

Almost every part of the continent has suffered since independence. No sooner had the Belgian colony of the Congo achieved it than it was plunged into war. A major intervention was mounted by the UN, which failed to resolve the crisis. The riches of Congo, which became Zaire under the kleptocrat Mobutu Sese Seko, were squandered. In recent years it has been the scene of a largely unreported continental war, involving armies from 11 nations. Another potential regional superpower, Nigeria, has been riven by civil war and coups. In 1967 the Ibos in the province of Biafra declared independence and war ensued for three years, during which at least a million civilians died of starvation, like, in all probability, this child (right).

The despotic rule of the Army commander Idi Amin in Uganda from 1971 to 1979 was ended by the intervention of the Tanzanian army. Then in the north child armies were raised for the Movement for the Restoration of the Ten Commandments of God led by Joseph Kibwetere.

Zimbabwe (Southern Rhodesia) saw a marathon guerrilla war after the white government declared independence unilaterally in 1965. This led to the rise to power of Robert Mugabe as prime minister of the properly independent country in 1980. In Angola civil war started when it gained independence from Portugal in 1975 – and only appeared to end with the death of the rebel leader of the UNITA movement, Jonas Savimbi, in 2002. In East Africa Somalia disintegrated into a running battle between warlords, despite UN and US intervention. Civil war tore Ethiopia and Eritrea apart. In Sudan the Muslim north has waged brutal war on the Christian and animist South. In West Africa, in Liberia and Sierra Leone especially, the clash of warlords involved hideous mutilations of their victims. The British sent a task force to the latter to establish order.

Civil war in Nigeria
Biafran rebel soldiers posing for the camera during their
attempt to form a breakaway state, 1968.

Revenge in Uganda

A Tanzanian soldier beside the corpses of three Libyans
(who were the allies of Idi Amin) in Kampala in April
1979 (above). The intervention of the Tanzanians ended
Amin's tyranny.

Antique guns
Firearms drill with the UNITA rebels in the early stages of
the Angolan War 1975-2002. Incredibly, most of the
weapons look to be muzzle-loaders.

Boy soldiers
One of the many child armies in Africa, this one in southern Sudan. Note the child nearest the camera is carrying a .303 Lee Enfield, as tall as himself.

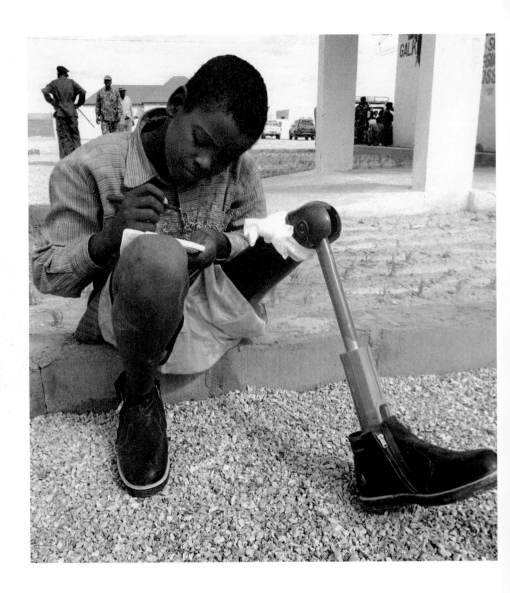

Land mine victim

Twelve-year-old Aweys Mohamed outside the Galkayo
Centre for Handicapped in Hargeisa, Somalia, July 1999.
He is a victim of landmines sown during the war against
the Somali dictator Mohamed Siad Barre, overthrown
in 1991.

America intervenes

US Marines searching a school for gunmen of the warlord
Mohamed Fara Aidid in Mogadishu, Somalia, April 1993.
Aidid's men later downed two American Blackhawk heli-
copters, killing 18 US soldiers.

Communism Cracks

I n August 1991 Mikail Gorbachev's rule in Russia had been threatened by a coup of old-style Communist officers. They detained him at his holiday home on the Black Sea, but did not know what to do next, so got drunk and the rebellion petered out. Its aftermath brought to power the flamboyant and less than abstemious Boris Yeltsin. In December 1991 the Soviet Union voted itself out of existence and the Communist era was at an end. The disintegration had on the whole been peaceful.

Yeltsin also was to face rebellion – from deputies in the parliament, housed in the White House. On 28 September 1993 he ordered parliament to be blockaded and then sent troops to storm the building and seize the television station on 4 October. In the south bigger trouble was breaking out. Georgia, now independent, disintegrated into a civil war. President Gamsakhurdia was driven from office in 1992, and apparently committed suicide in 1993. The centre of Georgia's capital is in flames during the fighting in 1992 (right). The former Soviet foreign minister Eduard Shevardnadze became president, and has survived several assassination attempts since.

In 1993 the people of the former Chechnya-Ingushetia pushed to break away under their charismatic commander Djohar Dudayev. Yeltsin ordered an all-out military operation against the Muslim rebels at the end of 1994. In early 1995 the capital Grozny was seized, though the Russians were mauled – they appeared to have forgotten the lessons of Stalingrad, though the rebels hadn't. In 1996 Dudayev was killed after his satellite phone had been traced by the Russians. In 1999 mysterious bombings in Moscow apartments were blamed on the Chechens who also made incursions into neighbouring Dagestan. They have shown resilience, operating from mountain bases, with secure training grounds, and with support across the Caucasus and in Turkey.

Assault on the White House

Tanks ordered in by Boris Yeltsin on 28 September 1993
to crush the parliament in Moscow (above). Vacuum
shells were fired at the White House which brought the
revolt to an end on 4 October 1993, killing dozens
(right). Troops also stormed the Television Station.

Grozny 1995
Russian Special Troops of
the Interior Ministry in
the Chechen capital,
which had been reduced
to rubble. Fighting would
erupt there again three
years later. The Chechens
had fought for the
Germans in large num-
bers in World War II.
Stalin then deported
them to Kazakhstan, but
under Khrushchev they
were allowed back, and
since then they have con-
sistently struggled for
their independence.

Air Attack
A Chechen rebel looks out for an incoming Russian plane
from the Presidential Palace in the centre of Grozny in
January 1995. His nationalist fervour contrasts with the
outworn international pretensions of the Communist
hammer-and-sickle.

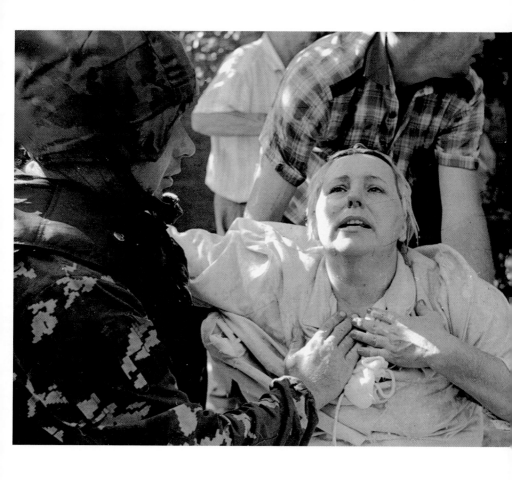

A hostage, a head

Hostages in the hospital at Budennovsk, Dagestan, seized
by maverick Chechen rebel, Shamye Basayev, in 1995
(above). About 20 people died, but Basayev got the
Russians to release his imprisoned fighters.

Death of Yugoslavia

I n 1980 President Tito died, and surprisingly his strange concoction of the six republics and two autonomous regions of the Federation of Yugoslavia lasted another ten years. In 1991 Slovenia, quickly followed by Croatia, declared independence. Slobodan Milosevic, the wily but crude dictator of Serbia, pretended to have none of it – though he had done a deal with the leadership of both. Slovenia went after a pantomime frontier war lasting a fortnight. Croatia suffered a terrible war for the last five months of the year. One third of Croatian territory was lost, in spite of the efforts of this Croatian officer, 'interrogating' a Serb in December 1991 (right).

In April 1992 the long-expected war in Bosnia broke out, where the Serbs, one third of the population, held two thirds of the territory. A UN force was sent to look on, and do little. The Serbs overran a UN guaranteed enclave of Muslims at Srebrenica on 12 July 1995. The Dutch garrison was too small to do anything, but witnessed the rounding up of about 7,000 Muslim males who were later shot out of hand in cold blood. It was the worst single atrocity in Europe since 1945. Eventually the Americans galvanised the UN and the European nations into action and under a brief bombing and artillery action on Sarajevo the Serbs agreed to peace at Dayton, which gave them 51% of Bosnia, though they still had a third, or less, of the population.

Dayton let Milosevic off the hook, and some of the participants at the conference were soon trying to do business with him. But by 1998 he was gearing up for another bout of ethnic cleansing in Serbia's southern province of Kosovo, where Serbs were outnumbered by Albanians nine to one. In March 1999 Nato began bombing to persuade him to desist. After 78 days his nerve cracked. He was out of office by October 2000 and on trial in the Hague seven months after that.

Massacre at Ahmici
A British soldier of the Cheshire Regiment serving with the UN stands guard over the ruined mosque at Ahmici in the Lasva valley, Bosnia. Some 109 men, women and children had been murdered here in a raid by Croat irregular thugs on 16 April 1993. As well as Serbs and Muslim Bosnians, there were plenty of Croats among the Bosnian population.

Race for peace

British paratroopers embark in helicopters to spearhead
the international peace force, KFOR, which went into
Kosovo on 12 June 1999. However, the Russians beat
them and got into Pristina the night before.

Paramilitary

In August 1998 Serb troops and police tried to recover towns and villages taken by the KLA in the Drenice plateau. Here a paramilitary policeman (MUP) watches burning hay ricks near the Serb stronghold of Orahovac.

WARS IN THE MIDDLE EAST

Neighbours and Nations

From the inception of Israel in 1948, the eastern Mediterranean has been close to war. In 1956 in the Suez crisis, Israeli tanks raced across the Sinai desert as the British and French went into Egypt. In 1967 Israel won a swift six-day victory by pre-emptive air strikes which destroyed most of the Egyptian air force on the ground and then drove to the Suez Canal, pushed the Jordanians off the West Bank of the Jordan, and the Syrians back from the Golan Heights. In 'Black September' 1970 King Hussein had to drive the Palestinians out of Jordan before they took it over. They moved to Lebanon where their presence was a major cause of the civil war which broke out in 1975. In 1973 the Arabs unexpectedly hit back in the Yom Kippur War – the Egyptians crossing the Canal and the Syrians driving down from the Golan. But due to swift defensive tactics, principally by General Ariel Sharon and Bren Adan in the Sinai, the Arabs were eventually checked.

In 1982 Israeli forces charged up Lebanon to Beirut – to fight the Palestinians who had been attacking the northern settlements in the Galilee region. Extrication from Lebanon would take another 19 years.

At home terror was growing too. Palestinians rose up in the First Intifada in December 1987. They then switched to suicide bombings. In 1997 another Intifada began, this time using bombs and bullets. A Palestinian is hit by a rubber bullet in a clash in Hebron in that year (previous page). In 2000, after Barak's peace offer was spurned, Ariel Sharon was elected Prime Minister on a ticket to crack down on the Palestinians. He is up against militants such as this 'shebab' on parade in Gaza, a supporter of Hamas (right).

In Algeria there had been a guerrilla war waged by the FLN against the French, with many atrocities committed on both sides, between 1954 and 1962, when de Gaulle granted the country independence.

War of Independence

Israeli soldiers firing over the walls at the Old City in
Jerusalem, 1948. The Arab states blocked a move at the
United Nations to make it an international city, with the
result that it remained divided between Jordan and
Israel until the Six-Day War of 1967.

Displacement

Refugees fleeing their villages round Gaza, 1948. An Israeli said at the time, 'You have no idea what happened in the Arab villages. It is enough that during the night several shells will whistle over them and they flee for their lives.' The claims of Palestinian refugees for rights of return and property rights are a fundamental grievance against the Israelis.

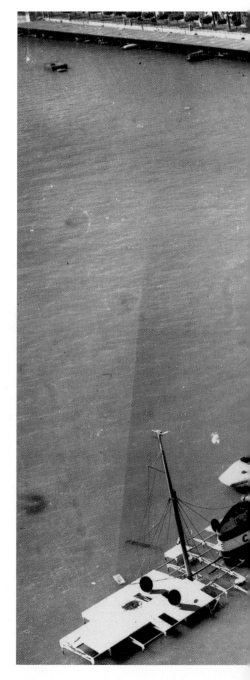

Canal in crisis
A ship sunk by Egypt to block the Suez Canal, 1956. It would not be cleared for more than a year. The British Prime Minister, Anthony Eden, believed that Colonel Nasser, the ruler of Egypt, 'would have his hands on our windpipe', once he had seized control of the Canal, since two-thirds of Western Europe's oil passed through it. This was the excuse for the Anglo-French invasion which led to the sinking of the block ships.

Suez operation

British soldiers digging in near Port Said in 1956 (above). The French and British intervention in Egypt was stopped by the Americans who threatened a run on the pound. Israeli troops checking Palestinians in 1956 in Gaza (right), which they had seized from Egypt during the Suez Crisis, because it had been used by Palestinian guerrillas as a base from which to mount raids on Israel.

Clash in Aden, 1967

Riots and fighting erupted in the British Colony of Aden as it was due to become independent. A demonstrator leaps through the flames shouting abuse at the British in the notorious Crater district (left). A Northumberland Fusilier dives for cover (above) as a grenade is thrown in Crater, where later 17 of his colleagues would be murdered and crucified by terrorists.

The French in North Africa

An old man comforts a child after the French Navy has
bombarded their home in the port of Bizerta after rioting
in 1961 (left). Tunisia had ceased to be a French protectorate in 1956, but they kept Bizerta as a base until 1962.
Security police in a riot in Algiers during the visit by
President de Gaulle in December 1960, which would
mean the end of French rule there (above). Car bombs
were used extensively for the first time by the insurgents,
and 84 were killed in the three days of de Gaulle's
visit alone.

Six-Day War

Israeli infantry going forward to the Suez Canal and prisoners being taken back to the rear in the Sinai in the lightning armoured strike in June 1967. The Egyptian prisoners have been deprived of their uniforms to discourage escape attempts. Note the markings on the bonnets of the Israeli vehicles, to aid identification from the air.

Suez ablaze
An Israeli officer observes
refineries blazing in Port
Suez after an artillery
bombardment in the Six-
Day War. He is on the
east side of the Canal.

Yom Kippur War
Israelis bringing in Egyptian prisoners of war after Israeli forces had retaken the west bank of the Suez Canal, October 1973. The war was no walk-over for Israel, with 5,500 dead and wounded and 800 tanks destroyed.

Golan Heights

An Israeli Skyhawk giving fighter ground attack support to Israeli troops recovering the Golan from Syrian armoured forces in the October 1973 War. For a few hours the Israelis lost control of the Heights.

Civil war, Lebanon

A woman desperately pleads for help for her husband
wounded during street fighting in the Dekawan district of
Beirut in 1975. For many decades before, the city had
been a cosmopolitan middle-eastern capital of pleasure.
You could ski in the nearby mountains or bathe in the
Mediterranean.

Heavy weaponry

A rocket fired from an army truck at a Falange position in an apartment block in the fighting between Palestinian, Muslim and leftist forces and the Falange Christian Militia in Beirut, in the first year of the 19-year civil war, 1975.

Intifada

A Palestinian hurling a sling shot in the opening phase of the First Intifada (the 'shaking'), which began in Gaza in the autumn of 1988. An image with strong echoes of the biblical encounter between David and Goliath.

Riot control

Israeli troops arresting a Palestinian boy in Hebron in the
Second Intifada, 1999. Such activity has inevitably had a
wearing effect on the image and effectiveness of the
Israeli forces, who have not adapted to urban guerrilla
warfare and riot control as well as they might.

Holding the line

Israeli frontier guards ranged against a crowd in
Ramallah, Second Intifada. Ramallah was shelled several
times and the Palestinian leader, Yassir Arafat, was
besieged there for six weeks in 2002.

Desert Storm

On August 2 1990 Saddam Hussein sent his armoured columns across the desert to seize Kuwait, which he claimed as the rightful 19th province of Iraq. His economy was in trouble, after the gruelling war against Iran from 1980 to 1988 in which there had been more than a million casualties.

Once he marshalled his forces, Saddam did not like to back down, though what he intended to achieve in grabbing Kuwait is not clear. President George Bush Senior assembled a coalition force of nearly half a million, including Egypt, Syria, the Emirates, Saudi Arabia, France and Britain. Most of the air force was provided by America.

The war in the Gulf in 1991 was old fashioned, but with a new twist. A huge assembly of armour was gathered in the desert. The air forces largely used 'dumb bombs' and only 20 per cent of their arsenal was 'smart' guided weaponry. (One of these missiles was aimed at what was thought to be a command bunker in Baghdad, but which turned out to be an air-raid shelter, resulting in 407 deaths. Iraqi schoolchildren visit it on the tenth anniversary, right.) The twist was the role of the television media, which reported bombing and action as it happened.

Saddam's forces fled Kuwait after a month of bombing and an Allied ground offensive of 100 hours. He remained in power, however, which left unfinished business. For the next ten years he thwarted UN attempts to prevent him building a new arsenal of mass destruction – though in 1998 the US and Britain bombed for four days the known installations in Operation Desert Fox. In 2002 the US and Britain insisted that Saddam make full disclosure of his weaponry, demanded by nine UN resolutions. He retorted with a classic display of brinkmanship.

Iran-Iraq War

An Iraqi soldier kissing a portrait of Saddam at the opening of the Iran-Iraq War in 1980 (above). Iraqi prisoners of war captured by Iran during the 1980-88 war (right). The position of the Iranian clergy, who had come to power on the fall of the Shah at the end of the 1970s, was much strengthened by the war, though Iranian losses were huge. The Iraqi army was kept well supplied with arms paid for by Saudi Arabia, Kuwait and the US, fearful of Iran's Islamic revolution spreading. The war ended in a stalemate.

Flight of the Kurds

In March 1991 the Kurds
in northern Iraq and the
Shi'ites round Basra in
the south staged ineffec-
tual rebellions against
Saddam Hussein – having
greatly underestimated
the strength of the forces
left to him after the war.
Hundreds of thousands
of Kurds were driven
into the mountains,
across an arc from Mosul
to the Turkish border at
Cizre, by Iraqi forces
using helicopter gunships
and tanks. Thousands of
refugees gathered along
the border – here they
are being fed under the
'Safe Havens' pro-
gramme led by Britain,
America and France in
April 1991.

Desert Sabre

An Egyptian armoured
personnel carrier explod-
ing a land mine as it leads
the charge into Kuwait
City in Operation Desert
Sabre, February 1991.

Biting the dust
An Egyptian soldier guards Iraqi prisoners in the Kuwait
desert, February 1991.

Gruesome freight

A destroyed Iraqi truck on the Basra road out of Kuwait, early March 1991.

Collateral damage

A US F-16 flies over the oilfields set ablaze by Saddam's
retreating troops, causing a huge environmental hazard. It
took eight months to put the fires out (above). An Iraqi
tanker sunk by the allies (top right),

Mine disposal
A US frogman attaches an explosive charge to an Iraqi mine
so it can be blown up without causing damage (above).

GROUND ZERO AND AFTER

Future Uncertain

September 11th was a supreme and terrible example of 'asymmetric war', when a weaker protagonist finds the weak point in a much more powerful and sophisticated enemy – David against Goliath. Osama bin Laden's al Qaeda had already perpetrated asymmetric acts of war against the US Embassies in Kenya and Tanzania in the summer of 1998 and with the bombing of the USS *Cole* by a dinghy packed with explosives in Aden harbour in October 2000. The 19 or so terrorists of the group led by Mohamed Atta knew how to hit the power points of America, its most potent finance and defence centres, by turning airliners full of innocent civilians into flying bombs (previous page).

The hunt for the al Qaeda network, its bases and its leader in Afghanistan led to war with its hosts, the hardline fundamentalist Taliban regime there. The Taliban and al Qaeda were ejected from power in Afghanistan, but the latter's influence stretches from central Asia though the rest of the Muslim world to the vociferous and dissident Islamic communities of Europe and even the US and Canada. By the beginning of 2002 the crisis was at the heart of three intersecting conflicts: in Afghanistan and Central Asia as far as the Caucasus, the renewed fighting between the Israelis and Palestinians, and the undeclared war against Saddam Hussein, posing with a rocket launcher (right). There was a growing fear that Saddam, still keeping UN inspectors at bay, might supply chemical and biological agents to al Qaeda, Hamas and Hezbollah. But few would back Washington in its call for war against him.

Any hope of a quick victory was fading. Quoting the old toast drunk by naval officers hoping for promotion in Nelson's time, a British general in the Gulf told journalists to be ready for 'a bloody war and a sickly season' in Bush's 'War against Terrorism'.

Pentagon

The damage done to the US military headquarters building in Arlington, Virginia on 11 September. It tran-
spired that the al Qaeda hijackers planned to seize five
planes – two to attack New York and the others to hit
the White House, Congress and the CIA headquarters at
Langley, Virginia. The Pentagon was hit because the
hijackers couldn't identify the White House in time. A
fourth plane crashed in Pennsylvania as passengers over-
powered its hijackers. The fifth plane failed to take off
due to mechanical failure.

World Trade Center

The scene at Ground Zero of what is left of the Twin
Towers two days after the attack, 13 September 2001.
The two planes that hit the Towers both had nearly full
loads of aviation fuel, which made their impact hugely
destructive.

Hot pursuit
Soldiers of the US 10th
Mountain Division
blowing a door off in
southern Afghanistan as
they hunt for al Qaeda
and bin Laden.

Into Kabul
A tank of the anti-
Taliban Tajik Northern
Alliance driving into
Kabul, past a woman
wearing a burka – a cus-
tomary concealing gar-
ment imposed by law
by the Taliban,
November 2001.

Uzbek charge
Uzbek militia loyal to
the anti-Taliban General
Abdel Rashid Dostom
charge into the assault.
He took over Mazar-I-
Sharif, where
fighting continued
through 2002.

Friends of al Qaeda

Demonstrators in Pakistan in support of Osama bin
Laden hold up his picture and wear his mask, adapted
from the cover of *Time* magazine.

Caged

Taliban prisoners in Shebargan, December 2001. Such men as these had tried, and largely succeeded in taking Afghanistan back to the 7th century AD, the time of Mohammed.

Jerusalem, Intifada 2
Israeli police firing grenades at rioters above the Western or Wailing Wall, Jerusalem. The Wall is the holiest of places for Jews, and the Dome of the Rock behind it, one of the holiest for Muslims.

Suicide Bomb

Walking wounded being escorted away from a suicide bombing in Israel. Religious martyrdom has always been a potent tool in political hands. There is Paradise for the bomber and a large cash present for his family, from Saddam Hussein of Iraq.

Busload of death

One of the worst bombings by a Palestinian in Tel Aviv.
Atrocities like this made Ariel Sharon order a major
Israeli armoured incursion into West Bank towns where
suicide bombers were believed to be recruiting
and arming.

Battle of Bethlehem
Israeli soldiers patrolling
in the old town of
Bethlehem, where civil-
ians, gunmen and clergy
were besieged in the
Church of the
Nativity, 2002.

Index

Picture acknowledgements

This book was produced by **getty**images Publishing Projects. We would like to thank the following for their assistance.

Bob Kopan/WarPage Collection 83 ITAR-TASS 374, 375, 379 National Photo Collection/The State of Israel 389, 390-1, 411, 438-9, 440, 441 Network Photographers Antony Suau 376-7; Roger Hutchings 382-3 **Press Association** 355, 370, 371, 410, 413, 418-19, 420, 421, 434-5, 442-3 **Reuters** Yannis Behrakis 432-3; Randy Belinsky 408-9; Malcolm Linton 346 **US Dept. of Defense** DoD DVIC MARB CA 82, 137, 145, 270, 422, 423t, 423b

All other images in this book are from Getty Images collections including the following which have further attributions:
George C. Beresford 10l; Felice A. Beato 60, 61, 62, 63; Harry Benson/Daily Express 348-9; Mathew Brady 34t, 35; David Brauchli 378; Paula Bronstein 18; Capt. James Burke 59, 64-5, 66-7; Larry Burrows/Daily Express 334-5; David Cairns/Daily Express 366; Charles Chevalier/George Eastman House 269; Patrick Christian 16; John Downing/Daily Express 369; Brian Eades/The Observer 342-3; Jack Esten 319; Roger Fenton 21, 22-3, 27, 28b, 29; Terry Fincher /Evening Standard 340-1, Terry Fincher/Daily Express 400-1; Alexander Gardner 33; Robert Giroux 424-5; Zvika Golan 17; Bert Hardy 322, 327, 328; M Haynes 100; Charles Hewitt 325, 395; Chris Hondros 429; Bob Houlihan 428; Roger Hutchings/The Observer 357; Imperial War Museum 148-9, 240; INA 427; Fenno Jacobs 317; Alan Jackson 306; Peter Jouvenal 360-1; Slava Katamidze Collection 12, 122-3, 157, 158-9, 160, 162, 163, 164-5, 166-7, 168, 169, 247, 250, 251, 255, 258, 259, 260, 302-3, 306, 308-9; David Knox 31; Library of Congress 32, 36, 37, 69b, 114, 241, 292-3; Malcolm Linton 373; Greg Marinovich 381, 386-7; Leonard McCombe 10r; William Lovelace/Daily Express 359; Tony McGrath/The Observer 358; Gaspar-Felix Nadar 46, 47; New York Times Co. 209; Oleg Nikishin 437; Paul O'Driscoll/ The Observer 363; Joe Raedle 430-1; Fred Ramage 296-7; RDA/Tallandier 234; William Rider-Rider 121; Thomas C Roche/Mathew Brady 38-9; Robertson 25; David Rosenblum 404; Robert F Sargent 290-1; Pascal Sebah 71; Scott Swanson Collection 263; Tom Smith/Daily Express 352-3; Marcus Sparing 26t; Russel Tadich 385; Reinhold Thiele 87, 88, 89, 90-1, 92-3; Visual News 436; Gavin Young/The Observer 368

For information about licensing Getty Images content contact your local Getty Images office or email liz.ihre@gettyimages.com